The COMPLETE BIBLE GUIDE *for Beginners*

ILLUSTRATED EDITION

VISUAL EDITION

INFOGRAPHICS, MAPS & FULL-COLOR ILLUSTRATION

Published by
GRAPEVINE BOOKS

www.grapevinebooks.com
email: grapevineindiapublishers@gmail.com

Ordering Information:
Quantity sales: Special discounts are available on quantity purchases
by corporations, associations, and others.
For details, reach out to the publisher.

First published by Grapevine Books, 2025

CONTENTS

BOOKS OF THE BIBLE

CONTENTS

BOOKS OF THE BIBLE

EXTRAS

WHAT IS THE BIBLE

The Bible is the sacred collection of writings inspired by God and entrusted to the Church. It tells the story of God's relationship with humanity, from creation to salvation in Christ.

The Bible is one unified story told through many books written over centuries. Different authors, cultures, and styles contribute to one divine message.

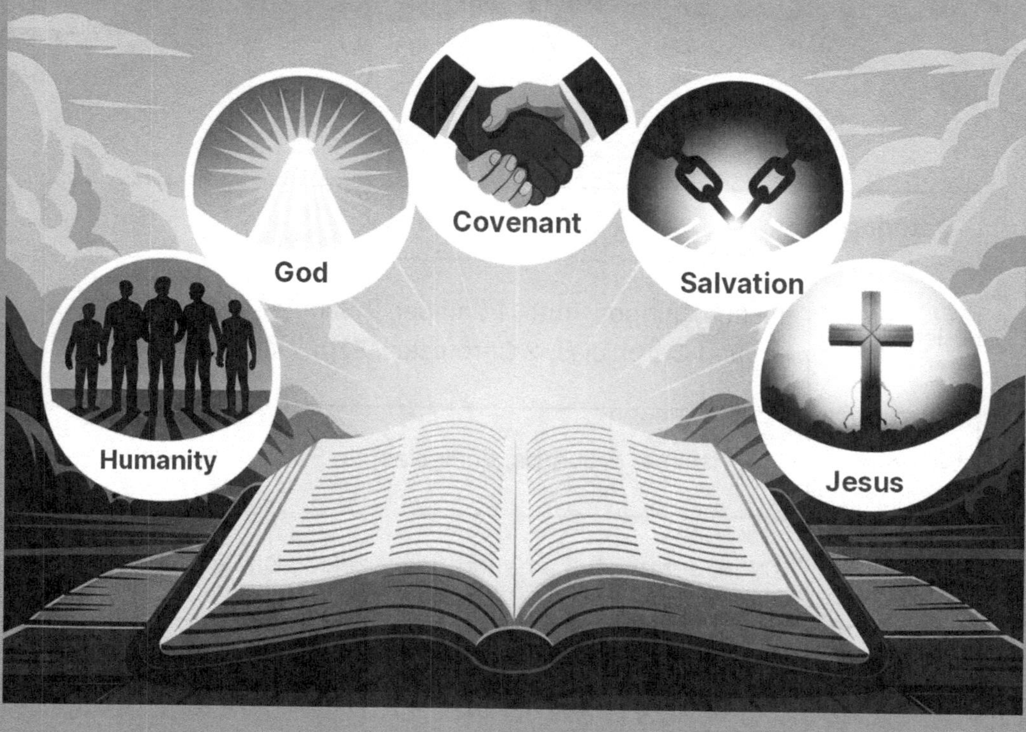

AT A GLANCE

OLD TESTAMENT

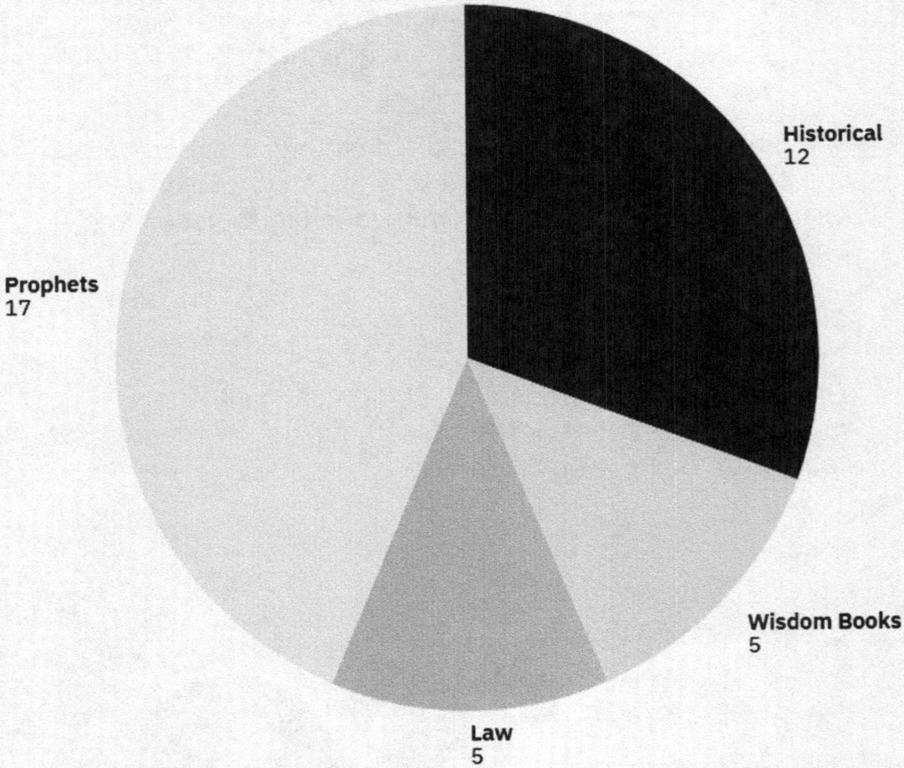

Category	Books
Historical	Joshua, Judges, Ruth, 1 Samuel, 2 Samuel, 1 Kings, 2 Kings, 1 Chronicles, 2 Chronicles, Ezra, Nehemiah
Wisdom	Job, Psalms, Proverbs, Ecclesiastes, Song of Songs
Major Prophets	Isaiah, Jeremiah, Lamentations, Ezekiel, Daniel
Minor Prophets	Hosea, Joel, Amos, Obadiah, Jonah, Micah, Nahum, Habakkuk, Zephaniah, Haggai, Zechariah, Malachi

OLD TESTAMENT

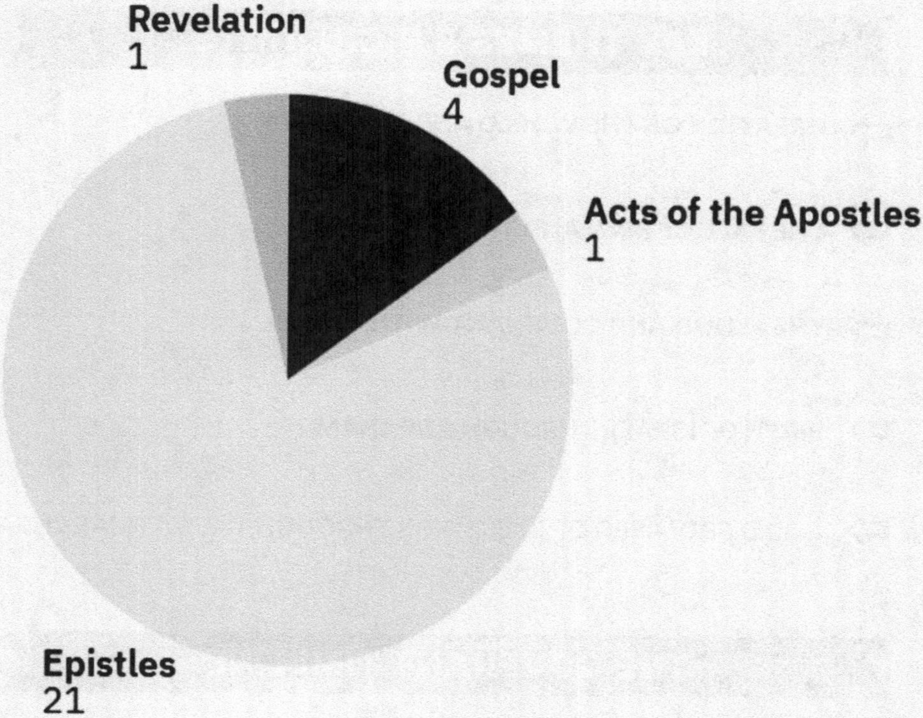

Category	Books
Gospels	Matthew, Mark, Luke, John
Church History	Acts of the Apostles
Epistles	*Pauline Letters* Romans, 1 Corinthians, 2 Corinthians, Galatians, Ephesians, Philippians, Colossians, 1 Thessalonians, 2 Thessalonians, 1 Timothy, 2 Timothy, Titus, Philemon *General Letters* Hebrews, James, 1 Peter, 2 Peter, 1 John, 2 John, 3 John, Jude
Revelation	The Book of Revelation

GENESIS

KEY THEMES & HIGHLIGHTS

- ⇨ CREATION OF THE WORLD AND HUMANITY
- ⇨ THE FALL OF MAN AND THE FIRST SIN
- ⇨ THE FLOOD AND COVENANT WITH NOAH
- ⇨ BIRTH OF ISRAEL THROUGH ABRAHAM
- ⇨ GOD'S PROMISES OF BLESSINGS THROUGH THE PATRIARCHS

THE COVENANT TIMELINE

Promise
God promises Abraham to make him a great nation.

Isaac's Birth
A miracle son is born to Abraham and Sarah.

Faith Tested
Abraham is commanded to sacrifice Isaac.

Jacob's Deception
Jacob receives blessing meant for Esau.

Joseph's Rise
Joseph's dreams lead to betrayal and his rise in Egypt.

CREATION TIMELINE

DAY 1

God created light, separating it from darkness, establishing day and night.

DAY 2

God created the sky, separating the waters above from the waters below.

DAY 3

God gathered the waters, revealing dry land; He created seas, land, and vegetation.

DAY 4

God created the sun, moon, and stars to govern day and night and mark seasons.

DAY 5

God created sea creatures and birds, commanding them to be fruitful and fill the earth.

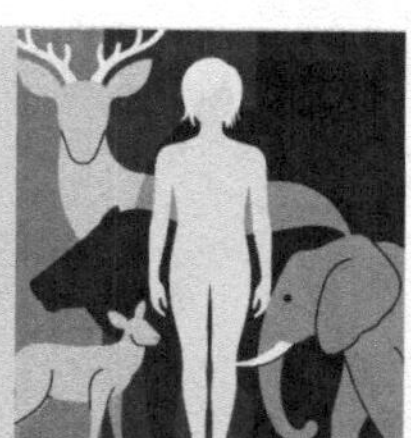

DAY 6

God created land animals and mankind in His image, giving them dominion over the earth.

DAY 7

God rested, sanctifying the seventh day and making it holy, completing His work.

EXODUS

KEY THEMES & HIGHLIGHTS

- DELIVERANCE
- LAW AND COVENANT
- GOD'S PRESENCE
- FAITH AND OBEDIENCE TESTED

THE COVENANT TIMELINE

Israel's Slavery
Israel is enslaved in Egypt for several generations.

Moses' Call
God calls Moses from the burning bush to lead Israel.

Ten Plagues
God sends plagues upon Egypt to convince Pharaoh to release Israel.

Red Sea Crossing
Moses parts the Red Sea; Israel escapes Egypt.

Covenant at Sinai
God gives Moses the Ten Commandments at Mount Sinai.

THE 10 PLAGUES

Water turned to blood

Frogs

Gnats

Flies

Livestock plague

Boils

Hail

Locusts

Darkness

Death

LEVITICUS

KEY THEMES & HIGHLIGHTS

- HOLINESS AND PURITY
- SACRIFICE AND ATONEMENT
- PRIESTLY DUTIES AND THE TABERNACLE
- COMMUNITY AND SOCIAL JUSTICE

MAJOR OFFERINGS

Sacrifice and Atonement.

Burnt Offering (Ola)

A complete offering burned to God as an expression of worship and devotion.

Grain Offering (Minhah)

A gift of fine flour, oil, and incense offered in gratitude to God.

Peace Offering (Shelamim)

Offered to celebrate peace and fellowship with God and community.

Sin Offering (Hattat)

Made to atone for unintentional sins and restore relationship with God.

DEUTERONOMY

KEY THEMES & HIGHLIGHTS

- ⇨ COVENANT RENEWAL AND OBEDIENCE
- ⇨ LEADERSHIP AND SUCCESSION
- ⇨ BLESSINGS AND CURSES
- ⇨ JUSTICE AND SOCIAL RESPONSIBILITY

BLESSINGS AND CURSES

Blessings Obedience

Curses of Disobedience

NUMBERS

KEY THEMES & HIGHLIGHTS

- ⇨ CENSUS AND ORGANIZATION
- ⇨ WILDERNESS WANDERINGS AND DISOBEDIENCE
- ⇨ GOD'S PROVISION AND FAITHFULNESS
- ⇨ LEADERSHIP CHALLENGES AND SUCCESSION

GOD'S PROVISION AND ISRAEL'S RESPONSE

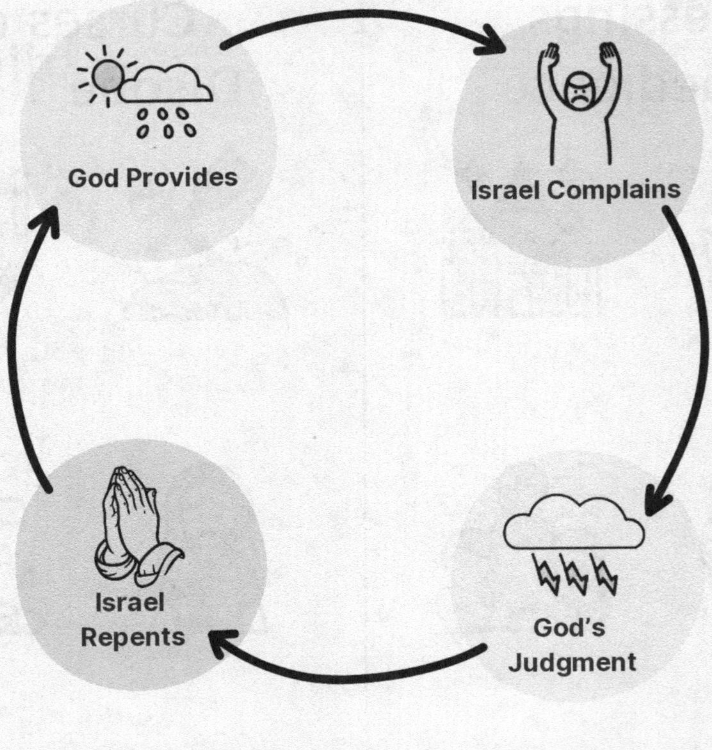

JUDGES

KEY THEMES & HIGHLIGHTS

- ⇨ CYCLES OF SIN AND REDEMPTION
- ⇨ GOD'S PROVISION THROUGH LEADERS
- ⇨ FAITHFULNESS AND DISOBEDIENCE
- ⇨ DIVINE INTERVENTION

THE JUDGES OF ISRAEL

Othniel

Ehud

Shamgar

Deborah

Barak

Gideon

Tola

Jair

Jephthah

Ibzan

Elon

Abdon

Samson

RUTH

KEY THEMES & HIGHLIGHTS

- ⇨ LOYALTY BEYOND BLOOD AND CIRCUMSTANCE
- ⇨ GOD'S PROVIDENCE IN ORDINARY LIVES
- ⇨ REDEMPTION THROUGH FAITHFUL OBEDIENCE
- ⇨ HOPE RESTORED THROUGH COVENANT LOVE

RUTH'S LIFE

Famine and Loss

Naomi loses husband and sons in Moab

Ruth's Choice

Ruth commits to Naomi and Israel.

Gleaning in Boaz's Field

Ruth encounters Boaz through her daily work.

Threshing Floor Appeal

Ruth seeks Boaz's protection, trusting in redemption.

Redemption & Lineage

Ruth and Boaz are forefathers of David and Jesus.

RUTH'S FAMILY TREE

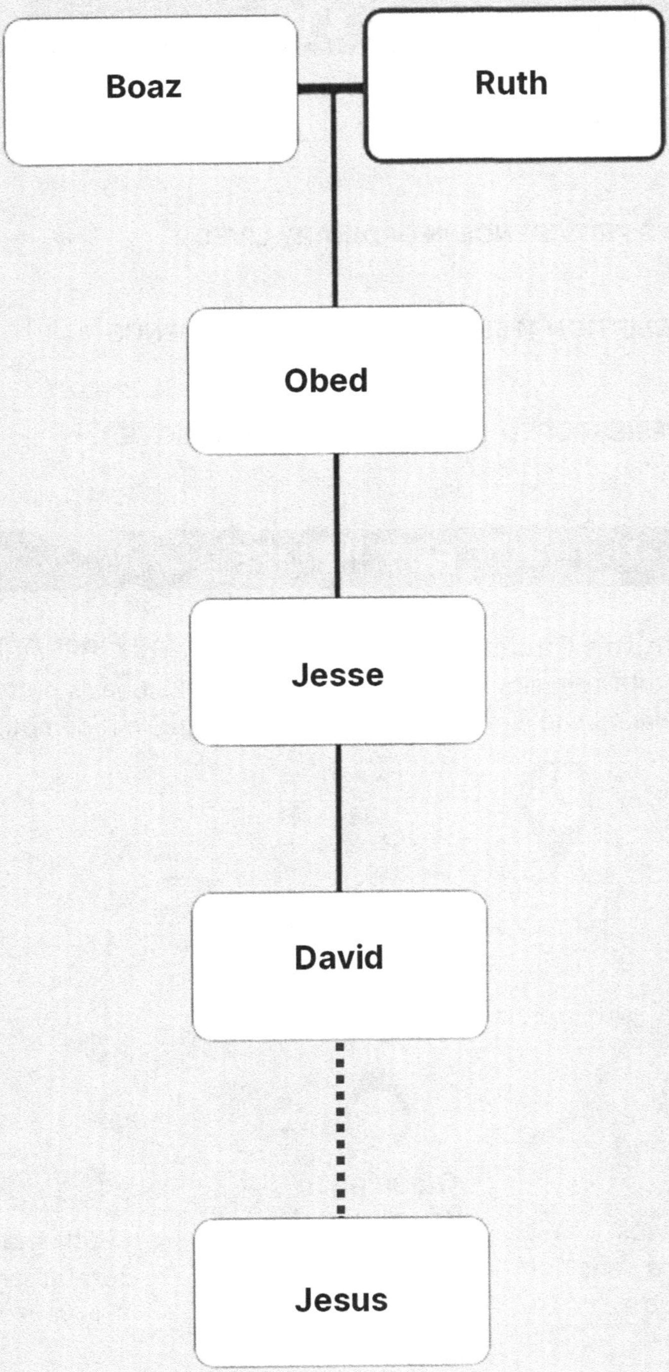

1 SAMUEL

KEY THEMES & HIGHLIGHTS

- ⇨ GOD'S AUTHORITY OVER HUMAN LEADERSHIP
- ⇨ OBEDIENCE MATTERS MORE THAN SACRIFICE
- ⇨ TRANSITION FROM JUDGES TO KINGSHIP
- ⇨ FAITHFULNESS TESTED UNDER PRESSURE

RUTH'S LIFE

Samuel Called by God

God establishes prophetic leadership.

Israel Demands a King

People reject God as direct ruler.

Saul Anointed King

First king, chosen by God.

Saul's Disobedience

Saul loses God's favor.

David Anointed

God chooses a future king.

FROM PROPHET TO KING

2 SAMUEL

KEY THEMES & HIGHLIGHTS

- GOD'S COVENANT FAITHFULNESS TO DAVID
- POWER BRINGS RESPONSIBILITY AND ACCOUNTABILITY
- SIN CARRIES LASTING CONSEQUENCES
- REPENTANCE RESTORES RELATIONSHIP WITH GOD

RUTH'S LIFE

David Becomes King

Unites Israel under one ruler.

Jerusalem Established

Political and spiritual center formed.

God's Covenant Promise

David's line established forever.

David's Great Sin

Failure with Bathsheba.

Restoration

Forgiveness granted, fallout remains.

THE LIFE OF KING DAVID

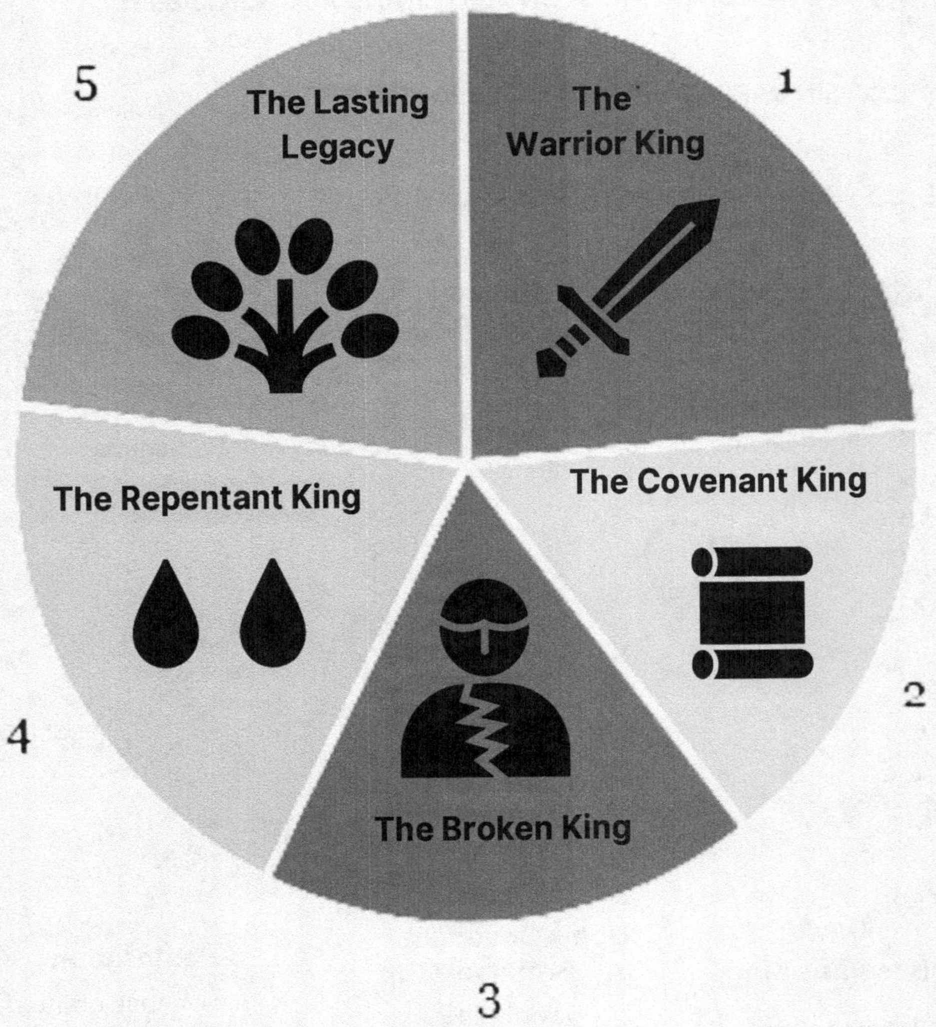

1 KINGS

KEY THEMES & HIGHLIGHTS

- WISDOM CAN BE LOST THROUGH COMPROMISE
- FAITHFULNESS DETERMINES A KINGDOM'S STABILITY
- DIVIDED HEARTS LEAD TO DIVIDED NATIONS
- TRUE WORSHIP VERSUS FALSE DEVOTION

RUTH'S LIFE

Solomon Crowned King
David's reign passes to Solomon.

Temple Built in Jerusalem
Center of worship established.

Solomon's Compromise
Foreign influences lead to idolatry.

Kingdom Divides
Israel and Judah separate.

Rise of Rival Kings
Competing kingdoms emerge.

THE DIVIDED KINGDOM

2 KINGS

KEY THEMES & HIGHLIGHTS

- ⇨ PERSISTENT REBELLION LEADS TO EXILE
- ⇨ GOD'S PATIENCE DELAYS BUT DOES NOT CANCEL JUDGMENT
- ⇨ PROPHETS SPEAK TRUTH TO FAILING POWER
- ⇨ GOD REMAINS SOVEREIGN OVER NATIONS

RUTH'S LIFE

Prophets Warn the Kings

Calls to repentance ignored.

Israel Falls to Assyria

Northern kingdom destroyed.

Judah's Temporary Survival

Kings alternate between reform and rebellion.

Jerusalem Falls

Temple destroyed.

Exile Begins

People carried into captivity.

PROPHETS AND
THE FALL OF KINGS
I. GOD'S
MESSENGERS
II. FAILING
THRONES
III. EXILE

1 CHRONICLES

KEY THEMES & HIGHLIGHTS

- ⇨ GOD'S COVENANT REMEMBERED THROUGH GENERATIONS
- ⇨ IDENTITY SHAPED BY SACRED HISTORY
- ⇨ GOD'S PROMISES PRESERVED DESPITE EXILE
- ⇨ JERUSALEM AS SPIRITUAL CENTER

RUTH'S LIFE

Genealogies of Israel
God's people traced through generations.

Rise of King David
God establishes chosen leadership.

Jerusalem Captured
City becomes national center.

Ark Brought to Jerusalem
Worship restored at the heart of Israel.

Temple Preparations
David prepares for future worship.

The Line of Promise
The Worshiping King
The City of God
The Unbuilt Temple
KING
DAVID
LEGACY REFRAMED

2 CHRONICLES

KEY THEMES & HIGHLIGHTS

- ⇨ FAITHFUL WORSHIP SUSTAINS THE NATION
- ⇨ OBEDIENCE BRINGS BLESSING AND PEACE
- ⇨ PRIDE LEADS TO SPIRITUAL COLLAPSE
- ⇨ GOD RESPONDS TO HUMBLE REPENTANCE

RUTH'S LIFE

Solomon Builds the Temple
Worship centered in Jerusalem.

Faithful and Unfaithful Kings
Cycles of obedience and rebellion.

Prophetic Warnings Ignored
Calls to repentance rejected.

Temple Desecrated
Sacred space corrupted.

Exile of Judah
The kingdom falls and the people are removed.

THE DIVIDED KINGDOM

Dates (BC)	Kingdom of the Israelites
1020–1000	Saul
1000–961	David
961–922	Solomon

Dates (BC)	Israel (North)	Judah (South)	Dates (BC)
922–901	Jeroboam I	Rehoboam	922–915
901–900	Nadab	Abijah	915–913
900–877	Baasha	Asa	913–873
877–876	Elah	Jehoshaphat	873–849
876	Zimri / Tibni	Jehoram	849–843
876–869	Omri	Ahaziah	843
869–850	Ahab	Athaliah	843–837
850–849	Ahaziah	Joash	837–800
849–843	Joram/	Amaziah	800–783
843–815	Jehu	Uzziah (Azariah)	783–742
815–802	Jehoahaz		
802–786	Jehoash		
786–746	Jeroboam II		

EZRA

KEY THEMES & HIGHLIGHTS

- ⇨ RESTORATION BEGINS WITH OBEDIENCE TO GOD
- ⇨ GOD REMAINS FAITHFUL AFTER EXILE
- ⇨ SPIRITUAL RENEWAL PRECEDES SOCIAL RENEWAL
- ⇨ GOD MOVES HEARTS OF FOREIGN KINGS

RETURN FROM EXILE

Decree of Cyrus

Permission granted to return.

First Return to Jerusalem

Exiles journey home.

Altar Rebuilt

Worship restored first.

Temple Reconstruction Begins

Building resumes amid opposition.

Temple Completed

House of God restored.

THE DIVIDED KINGDOM

586

Nebuchadnezzer

Babylon conquers Judah.

538

Cyrus of Persia

The degree of the return of the Jews. The Temple construction begins within 2 years.

521

Darius I

New king of Persia.
Haggai and Zechariah begin their prophetic ministry soon after.

515

Temple completed

The Jewish governor Zerubbabel oversaw its dedication. It was less grand than Solomon's Temple.

464

Artaxerxes I

New king of Persia.

458

Ezra

The scribe goes to Jerusalem, starts a spiritual revival and enforces Torah laws.

444

Nehemiah

The Israelites rebuild Jerusalem's walls under Nehemiah's guidance.

NEHEMIAH

KEY THEMES & HIGHLIGHTS

- ⇨ PRAYER FUELS COURAGEOUS LEADERSHIP
- ⇨ GOD REBUILDS PEOPLE BEFORE CITIES
- ⇨ COMMUNITY STRENGTHENED THROUGH SHARED PURPOSE
- ⇨ FAITHFULNESS PERSEVERES DESPITE OPPOSITION

REBUILDING JERUSALEM

Nehemiah's Prayer
Burden for Jerusalem formed.

Permission From the King
Authority granted to rebuild.

Walls Rebuilt
City defenses restored.

Opposition Overcome
Builders work and guard.

Covenant Renewed
People recommit to God's law.

JERUSALEM'S WALLS

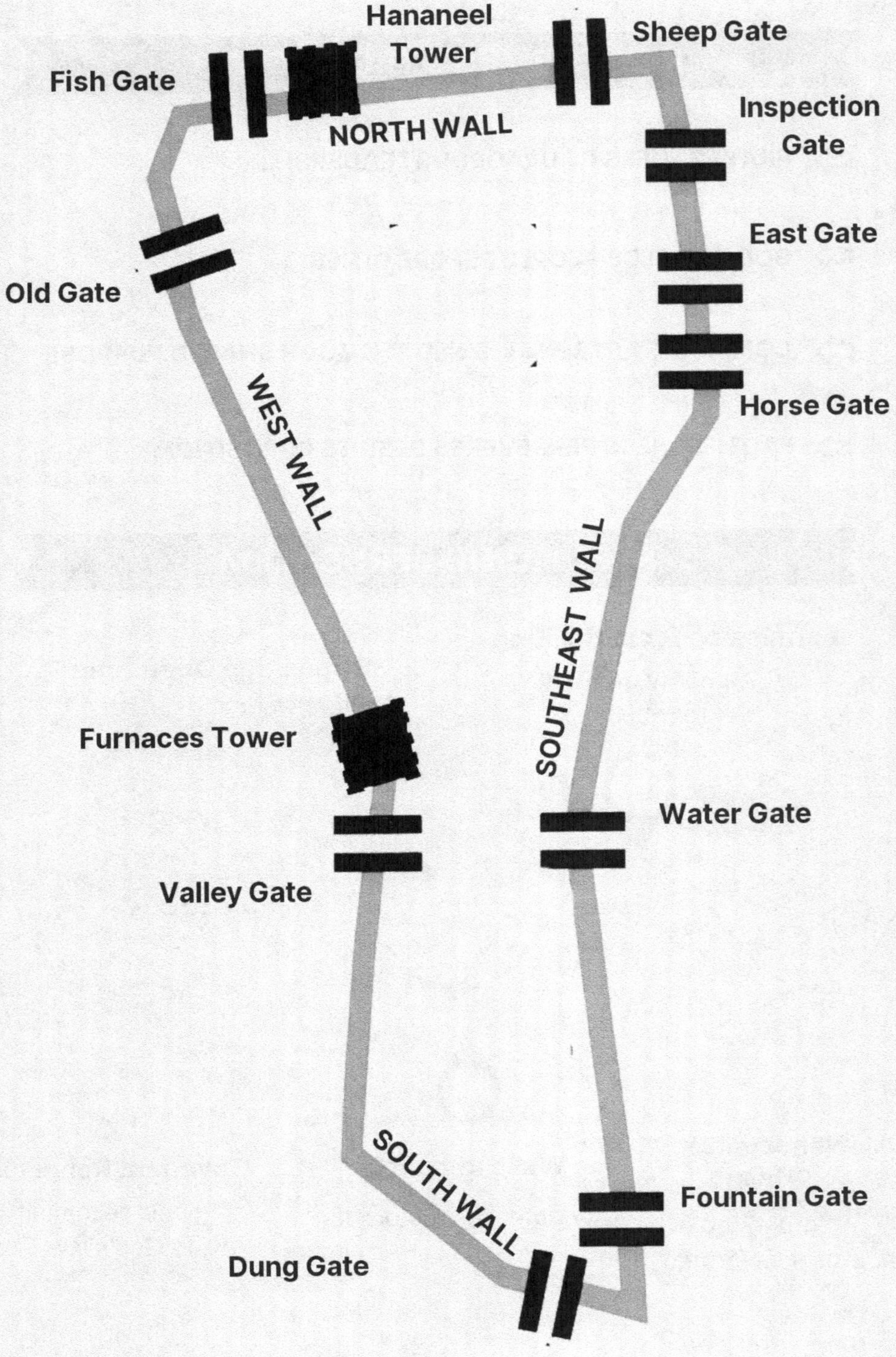

ESTHER

KEY THEMES & HIGHLIGHTS

- GOD'S PROVIDENCE BEHIND UNSEEN EVENTS
- COURAGE TO ACT AT DECISIVE MOMENTS
- DELIVERANCE EMERGES THROUGH FAITHFUL RISK
- PRAYER AND FASTING INVITE DIVINE INTERVENTION

JOURNEY OF FAITH

Threat Against the Jews
Haman plans the destruction of God's people.

Esther's Call to Act
Queen faces life-or-death choice.

Prayer and Fasting
People seek God's mercy.

Reversal of Fate
Haman's evil plans overturned.

Deliverance and Celebration
Sight restored, family renewed.

PURIM: CELEBRATING ESTHER

1

THE STORY

King Achashverosh chooses Esther as queen, unaware she is Jewish. Haman plots to destroy the Jewish people, but Esther reveals the plan and rescues the Jews.

2

THE MIRACLE

Purim's miracle unfolds through hidden events rather than open wonders. Courage and faith guide each step, showing how divine care works.

3

THE MITZVOT

Purim includes reading the Megillah, giving gifts of food to friends, helping those in need, and enjoying a festive meal. These acts strengthen generosity and gratitude within the community.

4

THE CUSTOMS

People dress in costumes, make joyful noise during the Megillah, and enjoy festive treats like hamantaschen.

5

THE NUMBERS

Purim is celebrated on the fourteenth of Adar. The Megillah has ten chapters, Achashverosh ruled 127 provinces, and the royal feast lasted 180 days, emphasizing the vast setting of the story.

JOB

KEY THEMES & HIGHLIGHTS

- ⇨ FAITH TESTED THROUGH UNDESERVED SUFFERING
- ⇨ GOD'S WISDOM SURPASSES HUMAN UNDERSTANDING
- ⇨ RIGHTEOUSNESS DOES NOT GUARANTEE PROSPERITY
- ⇨ LAMENT CAN COEXIST WITH TRUST

JOURNEY OF FAITH

Job's Righteous Life
Job lives faithfully, honoring God in prosperity and integrity.

Sudden Loss and Suffering
Children die, wealth destroyed, health taken.

Debates with Friends
Friends insist suffering proves hidden sin and guilt.

God Speaks from the Storm
God reveals His wisdom and sovereignty over creation.

Restoration and Renewal
Job is humbled and his blessings restored beyond former life.

THE GROWTH OF JOB

PSALMS

KEY THEMES & HIGHLIGHTS

- PRAYER EXPRESSED THROUGH EVERY HUMAN EMOTION
- GOD HEARS CRIES OF PRAISE AND LAMENT
- WORSHIP SHAPES TRUST DURING SUFFERING
- HOPE ANCHORED IN GOD’S ENDURING LOVE

AUTHORSHIP OF THE PSALMS

FORMS OF PSALMS

Joyful Praise — *Tehillah*

Spontaneous songs celebrating God's greatness, goodness, and works with joy and public worship.

Fear or Distress: *Tefillah*

Urgent prayers offered in danger, illness, or oppression, calling directly upon God for rescue.

Honest Lament: *Qinah*

Grief-filled prayers expressing sorrow, confusion, protest, and deep emotional pain before God.

Trust Renewed: *Miktam*

Reflective prayers expressing quiet confidence, protection, and growing trust in God's care.

Restored Praise: *Todah*

Thanksgiving praise offered after deliverance, celebrating God's faithfulness and answered prayer.

PROVERBS

KEY THEMES & HIGHLIGHTS

- DAILY CHOICES SHAPE LONG-TERM OUTCOMES
- RIGHTEOUS LIVING BRINGS LASTING STABILITY
- WISDOM BEGINS WITH REVERENCE FOR GOD
- WORDS REVEAL CHARACTER AND DIRECTION

DEVELOPMENT

Early Proverbs Collected
Solomon records short sayings teaching wisdom, discipline, and godly living.

Later Collections Added
Additional proverbs compiled by Hezekiah's scribes.

Solomon's Wisdom
God grants Solomon exceptional wisdom to lead Israel wisely.

Royal Instruction
Proverbs used to train princes, leaders, and future kings.

Wisdom for Daily Life
Proverbs preserved as practical guidance for every generation.

THE TWO WAYS

WISDOM
Honest, faithful
Ends in life, peace and honor
FOLLY
Prideful and short-sighted
Ends in loss and regret

ECCLESIASTES

KEY THEMES & HIGHLIGHTS

- ⇨ LIFE'S MEANING APART FROM GOD FALTERS
- ⇨ HUMAN STRIVING CANNOT SECURE FULFILLMENT
- ⇨ TIME GOVERNS ALL HUMAN EXPERIENCE
- ⇨ TIME GOVERNS ALL HUMAN EXPERIENCE

JOURNEY OF FAITH

Pleasure and Wealth Tested
Satisfaction proves temporary.

Time and Mortality
All share the same end.

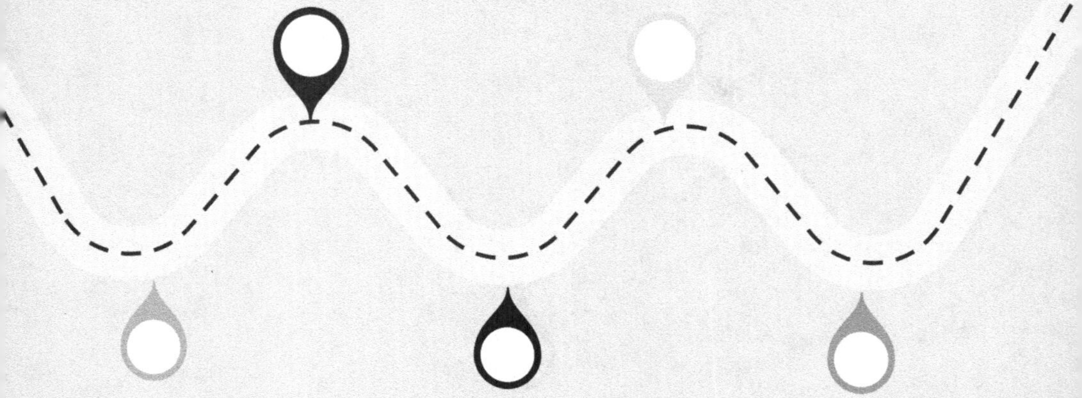

Human Toil and Achievement
Conclusion:
all is Endless labor.

Wisdom Compared to Folly
Wisdom helps but
cannot control life.

The Final Conclusion
Fear God and live wisely,
fearing judgement.

SONG OF SONGS

KEY THEMES & HIGHLIGHTS

- ⇨ LOVE CELEBRATED AS GOD'S GIFT
- ⇨ MUTUAL DESIRE EXPRESSED WITH DIGNITY
- ⇨ FAITHFUL LOVE REFLECTS DIVINE BEAUTY
- ⇨ COMMITMENT STRENGTHENS INTIMACY AND TRUST

JOURNEY OF FAITH

Pleasure and Wealth Tested
Satisfaction proves temporary.

Time and Mortality
All share the same end.

Human Toil and Achievement
Conclusion:
all is Endless labor.

Wisdom Compared to Folly
Wisdom helps but
cannot control life.

The Final Conclusion
Fear God and live wisely,
fearing judgement.

ISAIAH

KEY THEMES & HIGHLIGHTS

- GOD'S HOLINESS EXPOSES HUMAN SIN
- JUDGMENT CALLS PEOPLE BACK TO FAITHFULNESS
- HOPE PROMISED THROUGH A FUTURE MESSIAH
- GOD'S SALVATION EXTENDS TO ALL NATIONS

TWO WAYS OF UNDERSTANDING LIFE

Warnings of Judgment
Consequences are clearly declared for continued rebellion and corruption.

The Suffering Servant
Redemption is foretold through suffering, sacrifice, and obedient faith.

Call to Repentance
God confronts injustice and calls His people to return.

Promise of Restoration
God promises renewal and healing beyond coming judgment.

Future Glory and Peace
God's kingdom is revealed as just and everlasting.

AT A GLANCE

130

Prophetic messages of God's future promises

66

Chapters, making it the longest prophetic book

60

Years of ministry

KEY PROPHECIES AND FULFILLMENT

1. The Coming of the Messiah

He was wounded for our transgressions (Isaiah 53:4)

"But God commendeth his love toward us, in that, while we were yet sinners, Christ died for us." Romans 5:8 (KJV)

2. God's Servant, Israel

"But thou, Israel, art my servant, Jacob whom I have chosen." Isaiah 41:8 (KJV)

"Thou art my servant, O Israel, in whom I will be glorified." Isaiah 49:3 (KJV)

3. The Day of the Lord

"The day of the Lord is at hand; it shall come as a destruction from the Almighty." Isaiah 13:6 (KJV)

"And the seventh angel sounded; and there were great voices in heaven, saying, The kingdoms of this world are become the kingdoms of our Lord, and of his Christ; and he shall reign for ever and ever." Revelation 11:15 (KJV)

JEREMIAH

KEY THEMES & HIGHLIGHTS

- GOD'S WORD ENDURES DESPITE REJECTION
- JUDGMENT FLOWS FROM BROKEN COVENANT
- HOPE PROMISED THROUGH A NEW COVENANT
- GOD REMAINS PRESENT IN SUFFERING

TWO WAYS OF UNDERSTANDING LIFE

People Reject the Message
The people repeatedly refuse correction and ignore God's warnings.

Jeremiah Suffers
The prophet endures rejection while faithfully delivering God's message.

God Calls the Prophet
God places His word in Jeremiah to speak boldly.

Judgment Announced
Destruction is declared as a consequence of broken covenant.

Promise of a New Covenant
God promises renewed hearts and restored relationship beyond exile.

THE WEEPIING
PROPHET

LAMENTATIONS

KEY THEMES & HIGHLIGHTS

- ⇨ GOD'S WORD ENDURES DESPITE REJECTION
- ⇨ JUDGMENT FLOWS FROM BROKEN COVENANT
- ⇨ HOPE PROMISED THROUGH A NEW COVENANT
- ⇨ GOD REMAINS PRESENT IN SUFFERING

THE CITY OF JERUSALEM SPEAKS

LAMENTATIONS 1	AS A GRIEVING WIDOW
LAMENTATIONS 2	DIVINE JUDGEMENT IS DIVINE JUSTICE
LAMENTATIONS 3	A SUFFERER SPEAKS PERSONALLY, WITH ANGUISH AND HOPE
LAMENTATIONS 4	FORMER GLORY AND IMPACT OF THE SIEGE
LAMENTATIONS 5	COMMUNAL REPENTANCE AND PLEADING

EZEKIEL

KEY THEMES & HIGHLIGHTS

- ⇨ **REPENTANCE OPENS THE WAY TO RESTORATION**
- ⇨ **WISDOM FOUND IN GOD'S LAW**
- ⇨ **HOPE SUSTAINED DURING EXILE**
- ⇨ **GOD REMAINS FAITHFUL TO HIS PEOPLE**

RETURNING TO GOD

Responsibility Declared
Each individual is held accountable for personal faithfulness.

Dry Bones Revived
God promises national and spiritual restoration from total ruin.

Glory of God Appears
God's presence is revealed as powerful and unmistakably holy.

Judgment Explained
God's justice is shown as fair, necessary, and deserved.

New Temple Vision
Hope is expressed through restored worship.

DANIEL

KEY THEMES & HIGHLIGHTS

- REPENTANCE OPENS THE WAY TO RESTORATION
- WISDOM FOUND IN GOD'S LAW
- HOPE SUSTAINED DURING EXILE
- GOD REMAINS FAITHFUL TO HIS PEOPLE

RETURNING TO GOD

Pressure to Compromise

Kings demand loyalty that threatens faithfulness to God's law.

Kingdoms Rise and Fall

Daniel's visions reveal the temporary nature of earthly empires.

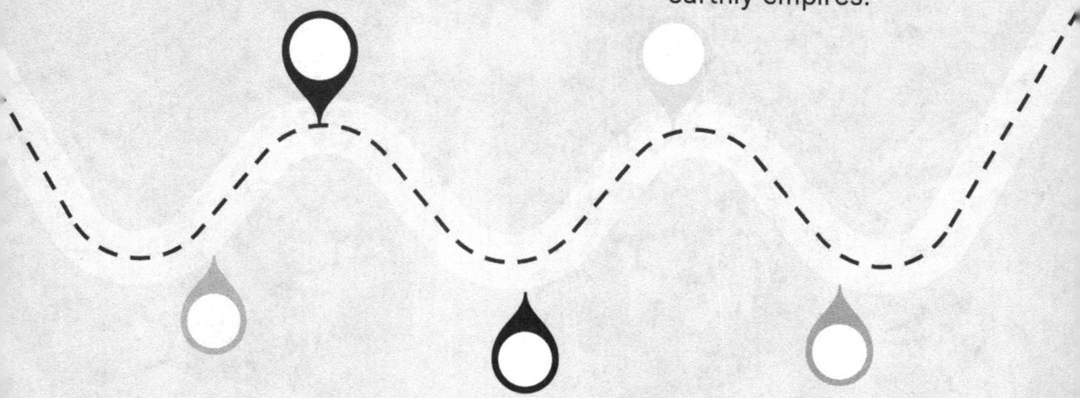

Faithful Living in Exile

Daniel and his companions obey God while serving in Babylon.

Divine Deliverance

God rescues the faithful from the furnace and the lions' den.

God's Eternal Kingdom

God establishes a kingdom that will never pass away.

HOSEA

CONTEMPORARIES

Northern Kingdom	Hosea, Amos
Southern Kingdom	Micah, Isaiah

RETURNING TO GOD

Called to Prophesy

God appoints Hosea to speak during Israel's moral and spiritual decline.

Marriage to Gomer

Hosea marries an unfaithful wife as a sign of Israel's unfaithfulness.

Children Named

God gives symbolic names announcing judgment, rejection, and broken mercy.

Israel's Repeated Unfaithfulness

Hosea buys back Gomer, showing God's enduring, restoring love.

Promise of Restoration

God promises renewed covenant love after repentance and judgment.

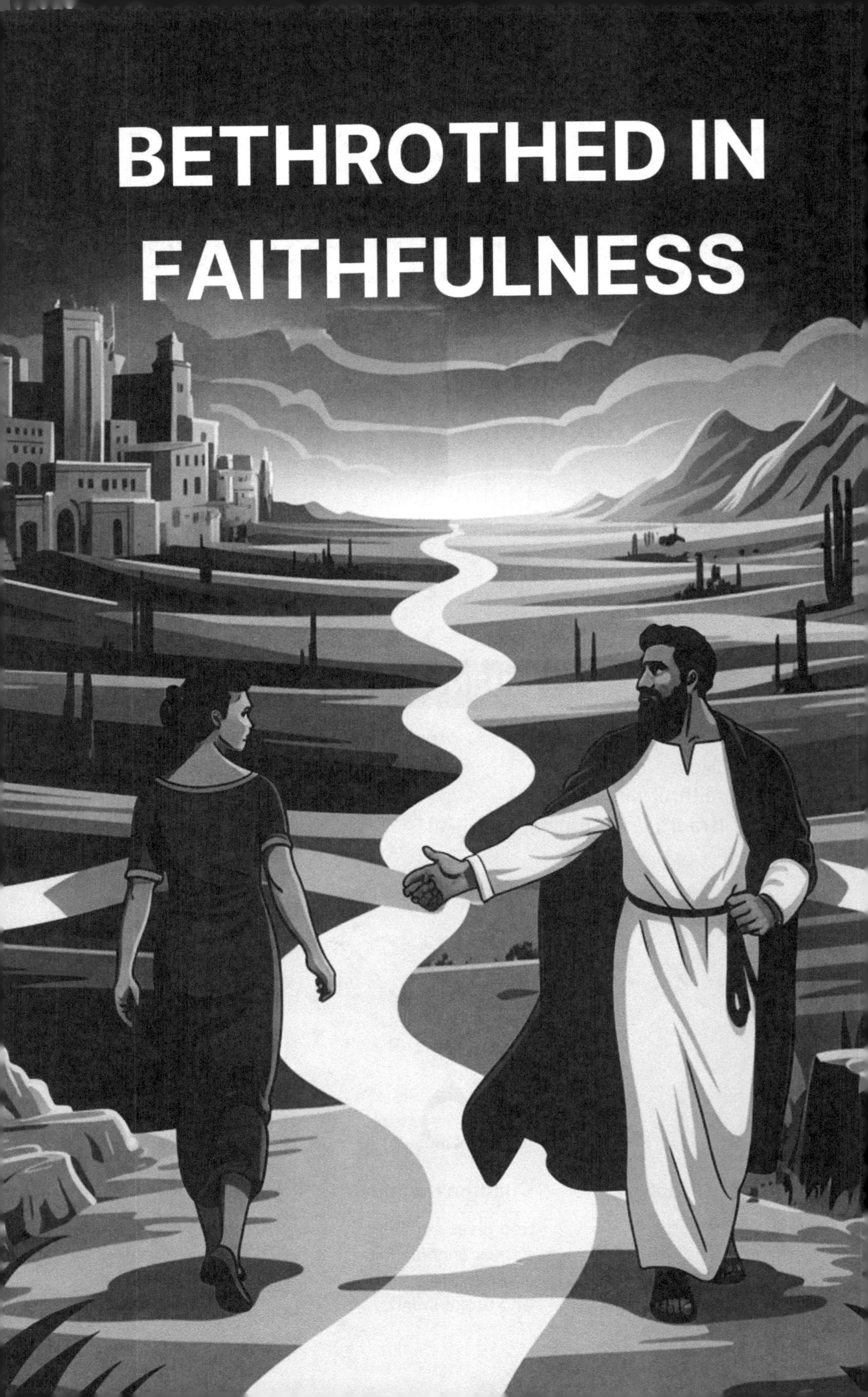
BETHROTHED IN
FAITHFULNESS

JOEL

KEY THEMES & HIGHLIGHTS

- JUDGMENT AWAKENS SPIRITUAL URGENCY
- REPENTANCE OPENS THE WAY TO MERCY
- GOD'S SPIRIT POURED OUT ABUNDANTLY
- HOPE FOLLOWS GENUINE REPENTANCE

RETURNING TO GOD

Disaster Strikes the Land
A devastating plague exposes spiritual complacency

Call to Repentance
God summons heartfelt national repentance, not empty ritual.

God Responds with Mercy
Compassion follows sincere turning back to God.

Spirit Poured Out
God promises renewed presence and power.

Future Hope Restored
Joy and abundance replace loss and devastation.

AMOS

KEY THEMES & HIGHLIGHTS

- JUSTICE DEMANDED OVER EMPTY WORSHIP
- GOD REJECTS HYPOCRISY AND OPPRESSION
- ACCOUNTABILITY APPLIES TO ALL NATIONS
- RIGHTEOUSNESS REFLECTS TRUE FAITH

JUSTICE AND ACCOUNTABILITY

False Worship Exposed
Religious acts fail without righteousness and mercy.

Call to Seek Good
Life is offered through repentance and justice.

Prosperity Without Justice
Wealth grows while injustice toward the poor increases.

God's Judgment Declared
God measures society against His standard of justice.

Hope Beyond Judgment
God promises restoration for a faithful remnant.

OBADIAH

KEY THEMES & HIGHLIGHTS

- ⇨ PRIDE LEADS TO INEVITABLE DOWNFALL
- ⇨ GOD DEFENDS HIS COVENANT PEOPLE
- ⇨ JUDGMENT MATCHES BETRAYAL
- ⇨ GOD'S JUSTICE IS UNAVOIDABLE

PRIDE AND CONSEQUENCES

Pride in Security
Edom trusts power and position rather than God.

Betrayal of a Brother
Edom rejoices over Israel's suffering.

Judgment Pronounced
Arrogance results in sudden and complete collapse.

Justice Reversed
What Edom inflicted returns upon itself.

God's Kingdom Prevails
God's rule ultimately replaces human pride.

JONAH

KEY THEMES & HIGHLIGHTS

- GOD'S MERCY EXTENDS BEYOND ISRAEL
- OBEDIENCE REVEALS GOD'S COMPASSION
- REPENTANCE INVITES DIVINE FORGIVENESS
- GOD'S MERCY CHALLENGES HUMAN PREJUDICE

DIVINE MERCY DEFIES EXPECTATIONS

God Sends the Prophet
Jonah is called to warn a foreign nation.

Prophet Flees God's Call
Resistance reveals fear and prejudice.

God Intervenes
Disobedience is confronted through discipline.

Nineveh Repents
Unexpected repentance leads to mercy.

God's Kingdom Prevails
God's rule ultimately replaces human pride.

MICAH

KEY THEMES & HIGHLIGHTS

- GOD DEMANDS JUSTICE OVER EMPTY RELIGION
- LEADERS HELD ACCOUNTABLE FOR CORRUPTION
- MESSIAH PROMISED FROM HUMBLE ORIGINS
- FAITH EXPRESSED THROUGH JUSTICE AND HUMILITY

JUDGMENT AND HOPE INTERWOVEN

Judgment Declared on Cities
Samaria and Jerusalem face consequences for rebellion.

True Faith Defined
God requires justice, mercy, and humble obedience.

Injustice and Corruption Exposed
Leaders exploit people and distort justice.

A Promised Ruler
A future shepherd-king is promised from David's line.

Future Peace Promised
Nations will live securely under God's righteous rule.

NAHUM

KEY THEMES & HIGHLIGHTS

- GOD'S JUSTICE CONFRONTS BRUTAL EMPIRES
- OPPRESSION DOES NOT ESCAPE DIVINE JUDGMENT
- GOD PROTECTS THOSE WHO TRUST HIM
- VIOLENCE ULTIMATELY DESTROYS ITSELF

THE FALL OF NINEVEH

God Declares Judgment
God announces punishment for relentless violence and arrogance.

Oppression Comes to an End
Nations are freed from Assyrian domination.

Cruelty Remembered
Assyria dominates nations through terror, conquest, and brutality.

Nineveh's Defenses Collapse
Military strength fails when judgment arrives.

God's Justice Affirmed
God proves faithful to defend the oppressed.

HABAKKUK

KEY THEMES & HIGHLIGHTS

- ⇨ **FAITH WRESTLES HONESTLY WITH INJUSTICE**
- ⇨ **GOD'S PLANS UNFOLD BEYOND HUMAN UNDERSTANDING**
- ⇨ **THE RIGHTEOUS LIVE BY FAITH**
- ⇨ **TRUST REMAINS DESPITE UNANSWERED QUESTIONS**

A DIALOGUE BETWEEN PROPHET AND GOD

Habakkuk Questions
The prophet challenges God about unchecked injustice.

God Reveals Judgment
God explains He will use Babylon as judgment.

Prophet Struggles with God's Answer
God's solution raises deeper moral concerns.

God Affirms His Sovereignty
God assures justice will prevail in time.

Faith Chosen Despite Uncertainty
Trust replaces fear as the righteous live by faith.

ZEPHANIAH

KEY THEMES & HIGHLIGHTS

- THE DAY OF THE LORD APPROACHES
- JUDGMENT PURIFIES GOD'S PEOPLE
- HUMILITY LEADS TO REFUGE
- RESTORATION FOLLOWS REPENTANCE

FROM JUDGMENT TO RENEWAL

Warning
God announces coming judgment upon all nations.

Condemnation
Idolatry and injustice are directly confronted.

Call
The faithful are urged to seek refuge in God.

Judgement
Evil is removed through divine action.

Restoration
God rejoices over a renewed and faithful people.

HAGGAI

KEY THEMES & HIGHLIGHTS

- ⇨ GOD'S PRIORITIES OUTWEIGH PERSONAL COMFORT
- ⇨ OBEDIENCE LEADS TO RENEWED BLESSING
- ⇨ GOD'S PRESENCE GIVES PURPOSE TO WORK
- ⇨ FAITHFULNESS REBUILDS COMMUNITY

REBUILDING GOD'S HOME

Misplaced Focus
Comfort is prioritized over worship.

Confrontation
The prophet calls attention to spiritual neglect.

Reconstruction
The people respond with renewed obedience.

Promise of Presence
Assurance replaces discouragement.

Restoration
God promises greater glory ahead.

ZECHARIAH

KEY THEMES & HIGHLIGHTS

- GOD ENCOURAGES REBUILDING THROUGH HOPE
- REPENTANCE OPENS THE WAY TO RESTORATION
- GOD'S PLANS EXTEND BEYOND THE PRESENT
- MESSIANIC HOPE STRENGTHENS WEARY PEOPLE

VISIONS OF RESTORATION

Visions of Protection
God reveals plans for Jerusalem's future.

God's Spirit Empowers the Work
Success comes through God's Spirit, not strength.

Call to Return to God
God invites repentance and renewed faithfulness.

Promise of Humble King
A peaceful Messiah is foretold.

Future Peace
God promises lasting peace and security.

MALACHI

KEY THEMES & HIGHLIGHTS

- FAITH GROWS COLD WITHOUT SINCERE DEVOTION
- GOD DESIRES FAITHFUL WORSHIP AND INTEGRITY
- COVENANT FAITHFULNESS RENEWS RELATIONSHIPS
- GOD'S JUSTICE WILL ULTIMATELY PREVAIL

CALLING A WEARY PEOPLE BACK

Spiritual Apathy Exposed
Worship becomes routine and careless.

Covenant Failures Confronted
Unfaithfulness spreads through community life.

God Calls for Genuine Return
Repentance is invited, not forced.

Coming Messenger
God prepares His people for renewal.

Hope
God's purposes remain unchanged.

THE FOUR GOSPELS

KEY THEMES & HIGHLIGHTS

- ONE SAVIOR, FOUR PERSPECTIVES
- GOSPEL: MEANING GOOD NEWS
- TOGETHER: COMPLETE PORTRAIT OF JESUS

MATTHEW

Written by: A former tax collector chosen as an apostle
Audience: Jewish believers
Focus: Jesus as the foretold Messiah
Detail: Frequent mention of the Kingdom of Heaven

MARK

Written by: Associate of Peter and a companion of Paul
Audience: Early Christians, especially Gentiles
Focus: Jesus' powerful actions that reveal His divine authority
Detail: Brief and fast-paced

LUKE

Written by: A physician and trusted companion of Paul
Audience: Gentile readers and seekers of faith
Focus: Jesus' compassion
Detail: Unique record of Jesus as a child in the Temple

JOHN

Written by: An apostle
Audience: Believers seeking deeper understanding
Focus: Jesus' divine identity
Detail: The famous "I am" statements, and washing the apostles' feet

MATTHEW

KEY THEMES & HIGHLIGHTS

- JESUS FULFILLS ISRAEL'S MESSIANIC HOPES
- GOD'S KINGDOM REVEALED THROUGH OBEDIENCE
- JESUS AS TEACHER AND KING
- DISCIPLESHIP REQUIRES FAITHFUL ACTION

JESUS THE PROMISED KING

Messiah Born from David's Line

Jesus is presented as the promised king of Israel.

Kingdom Teaching Proclaimed

Jesus teaches God's law with divine authority.

Miracles Performed

Miracles confirm Jesus' authority and compassion.

Rejection and Crucifixion

The king is rejected and suffers for His people.

Commission

Jesus rises and sends disciples to all nations.

MARK

KEY THEMES & HIGHLIGHTS

- ⇨ JESUS REVEALED THROUGH ACTION AND POWER
- ⇨ THE SUFFERING MESSIAH MISUNDERSTOOD
- ⇨ DISCIPLESHIP INVOLVES SACRIFICE AND FAITH
- ⇨ GOD'S KINGDOM ARRIVES WITH URGENCY

THE SERVANT IN ACTION

Public Ministry

Jesus moves quickly, preaching and healing.

Authority Displayed through Miracles

Evil and illness submit to His power.

Miracles Performed

Miracles confirm Jesus' authority and compassion.

Identity Questioned and Revealed

Jesus is revealed as Messiah through suffering.

Resurrection Announced

Victory over death confirms Jesus' identity.

LUKE

KEY THEMES & HIGHLIGHTS

- GOD'S SALVATION OFFERED TO ALL PEOPLE
- COMPASSION DEFINES GOD'S KINGDOM
- THE MARGINALIZED RECEIVE DIVINE ATTENTION
- THE HOLY SPIRIT GUIDES GOD'S PLAN

SALVATION FOR ALL

Compassionate Teaching
Outcasts and sinners are welcomed.

Journey to Jerusalem
God's grace is explained through everyday stories.

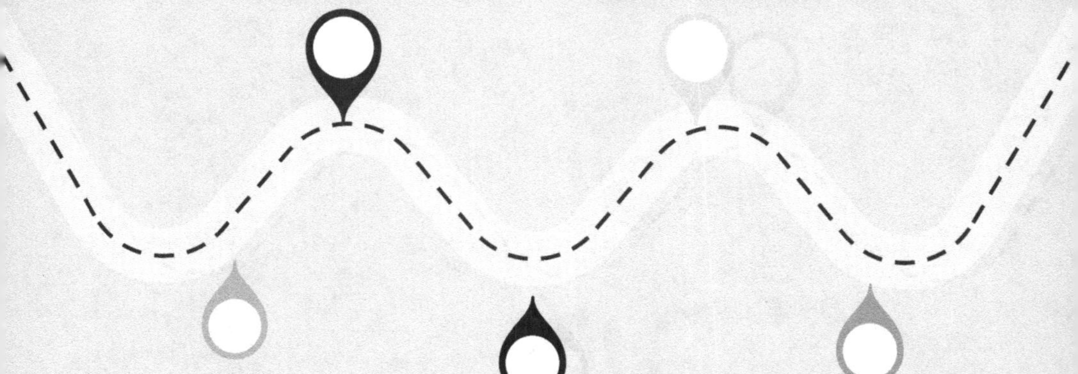

Miracle Births
God begins salvation through humble beginnings.

Parables
God's grace is explained through everyday stories.

Joyful Witness
Jesus moves knowingly toward suffering.

JOHN

KEY THEMES & HIGHLIGHTS

- JESUS REVEALED AS ETERNAL WORD
- BELIEF LEADS TO ETERNAL LIFE
- SIGNS POINT TO DIVINE IDENTITY
- LOVE DEFINES TRUE DISCIPLESHIP

SIGNS THAT REVEAL GLORY

Signs Reveal Glory

Miracles reveal divine identity.

Sacrificial Love Displayed

Love is fully shown through the cross.

Word Becomes Flesh

Jesus is revealed as God among humanity.

Faith and Opposition

Belief and rejection increase side by side.

Resurrection Confirmed

Jesus conquers death and grants eternal life.

ACTS

KEY THEMES & HIGHLIGHTS

- ⇨ THE HOLY SPIRIT EMPOWERS BELIEVERS
- ⇨ THE CHURCH MOVES FROM JERUSALEM TO THE NATIONS
- ⇨ WITNESS GROWS DESPITE OPPOSITION
- ⇨ GOD DIRECTS THE MISSION THROUGH PEOPLE AND EVENTS

JERUSALEM TO THE ENDS OF THE EARTH

Jerusalem as the Launch Point
Peter, John, and the apostles proclaim Jesus openly.

Gospel to the Gentiles
Cornelius receives the Holy Spirit, confirming God's plan for all nations.

Pentecost

The Holy Spirit comes upon the apostles, and the church is born

Persecution

Believers flee Jerusalem, carrying the gospel.

Paul's Missionary Journeys

Paul travels, plants churches, and eventually reaches Rome.

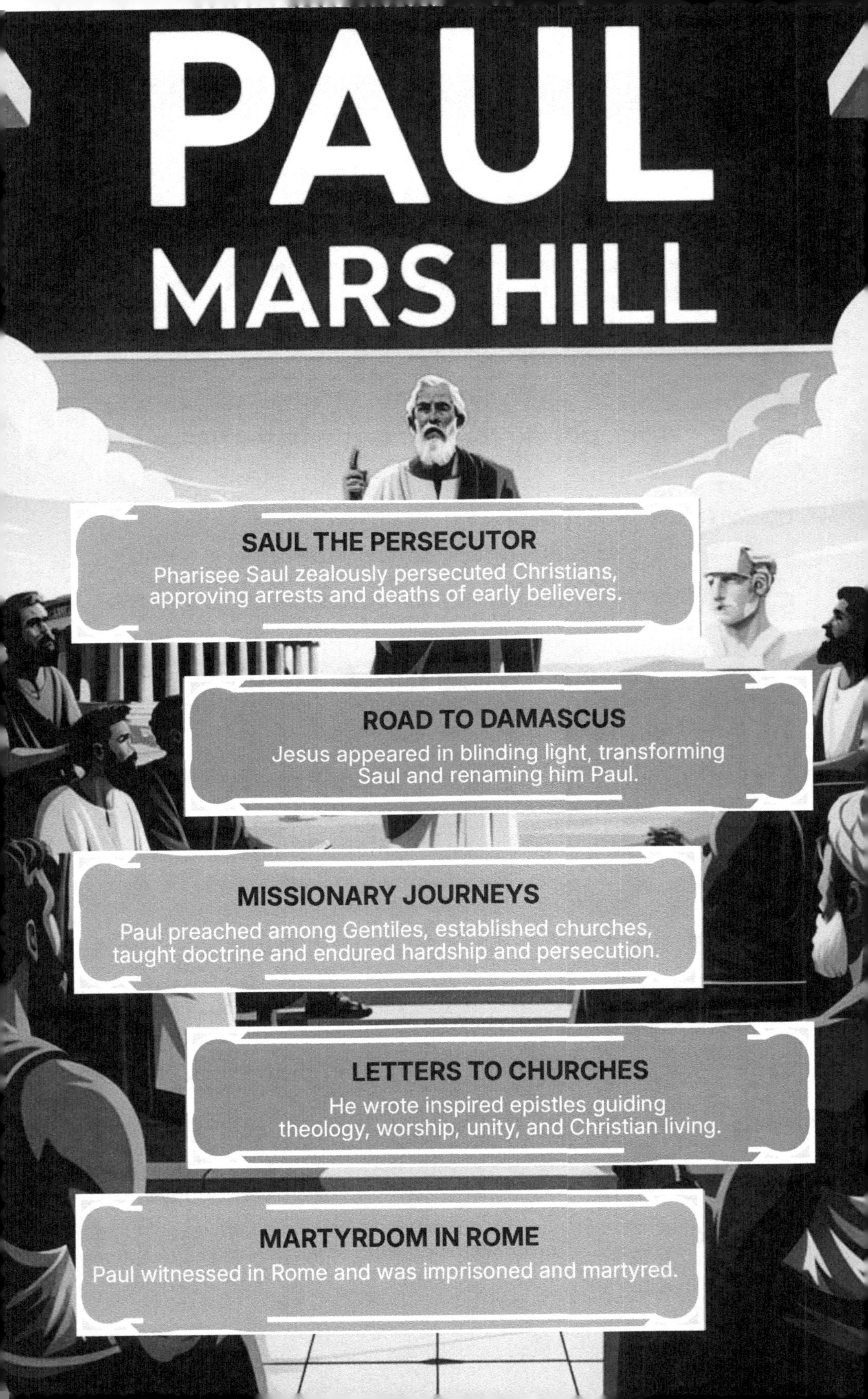
PAUL
MARS HILL
SAUL THE PERSECUTOR
Pharisee Saul zealously persecuted Christians, approving arrests and deaths of early believers.
ROAD TO DAMASCUS
Jesus appeared in blinding light, transforming Saul and renaming him Paul.
MISSIONARY JOURNEYS
Paul preached among Gentiles, established churches, taught doctrine and endured hardship and persecution.
LETTERS TO CHURCHES
He wrote inspired epistles guiding theology, worship, unity, and Christian living.
MARTYRDOM IN ROME
Paul witnessed in Rome and was imprisoned and martyred.

ROMANS

KEY THEMES & HIGHLIGHTS

- SALVATION BY FAITH ALONE
- UNIVERSAL NEED FOR GRACE
- RIGHTEOUSNESS THROUGH CHRIST
- LIFE TRANSFORMED BY THE SPIRIT

THE LOGIC OF SALVATION

Humanity's Sin

All people fall short of God's righteousness.

Faith in Christ

Justification comes through faith, not the law.

Life in the Spirit

Believers are freed from sin's power.

God's Plan for Israel

God's promises remain faithful.

Living Sacrifices

Faith produces obedient, transformed lives.

1 CORINTHIANS

KEY THEMES & HIGHLIGHTS

- ⇨ UNITY IN THE CHURCH
- ⇨ HOLINESS IN DAILY LIFE
- ⇨ LOVE AS THE HIGHEST VIRTUE
- ⇨ ORDER IN WORSHIP

BUILDING A HEALTHY CHURCH

Correcting Moral Failure
Believers are called to holiness.

Love Above All
Love gives meaning to every gift.

Christ as the Foundation
The Church belongs to Christ alone.

Spiritual Gifts for Service
Gifts serve the whole body.

Hope of Resurrection
Christ's resurrection guarantees eternal life.

2 CORINTHIANS

KEY THEMES & HIGHLIGHTS

- STRENGTH THROUGH WEAKNESS
- AUTHENTIC MINISTRY
- COMFORT IN SUFFERING
- FAITHFUL GENEROSITY

POWER THROUGH WEAKNESS

Defending True Apostleship

Paul explains his ministry's sincerity.

Generous Giving

Giving reflects God's grace.

Affliction and Comfort

God comforts those who suffer.

New Covenant Ministry

The Spirit brings lasting transformation.

God's Power Displayed

God's strength shines through weakness.

GALATIANS

KEY THEMES & HIGHLIGHTS

- FREEDOM IN CHRIST
- GRACE OVER LAW
- LIFE LED BY THE SPIRIT
- UNITY AMONG BELIEVERS

FROM LAW TO FREEDOM

False Gospel Confronted
Salvation cannot be earned.

Justification by Faith
Faith alone saves.

Freedom from the Law
Believers are no longer bound.

Walking by the Spirit
The Spirit shapes daily living.

New Identity in Christ
All are one in Christ Jesus.

PHILIPPIANS

KEY THEMES & HIGHLIGHTS

- JOY IN CHRIST
- HUMILITY AND SERVICE
- FAITHFULNESS IN HARDSHIP
- CHRIST-CENTERED LIVING

JOY IN EVERY CIRCUMSTANCE

Christ's Humility
Jesus empties Himself, becoming obedient to death on a cross.

Strength Through Christ
Contentment comes from Christ's power, not circumstances.

Joy from Prison
Paul writes from imprisonment in Rome, rejoicing despite suffering.

Unity Through Humility
Believers are called to serve one another.

Joyful Perseverance
Believers reflect Christ through unity and obedience.

COLOSSIANS

KEY THEMES & HIGHLIGHTS

- ⇨ CHRIST'S SUPREMACY
- ⇨ FREEDOM FROM FALSE TEACHING
- ⇨ NEW LIFE IN CHRIST
- ⇨ HOLY LIVING

CHRIST ABOVE ALL

Creator and Sustainer
All things exist through Him.

False Teaching Rejected
Human rules cannot save.

Christ the Image of God
Jesus reveals God fully.

Head of the Church
Christ leads and unites believers.

Living the New Life
Believers reflect Christ in daily conduct.

1 THESSALONIANS

KEY THEMES & HIGHLIGHTS

- HOPE IN CHRIST'S RETURN
- FAITH UNDER PERSECUTION
- HOLY LIVING
- ENCOURAGEMENT

LIVING IN HOPE

Joy Despite Suffering
Believers endure persecution.

Christ Will Return
The Lord will come again.

Faithful Witness in Thessalonica
The church spreads the gospel boldly.

Encouragement for the Church
Paul strengthens their faith.

Live Ready
Believers stay alert and faithful.

2 THESSALONIANS

KEY THEMES & HIGHLIGHTS

- ENDURANCE UNDER PERSECUTION
- GOD'S COMING JUSTICE
- TRUTH ABOUT THE LORD'S RETURN
- FAITHFUL DAILY RESPONSIBILITY

STANDING FIRM UNTIL THE END

Justice Will Come
God will repay oppression fairly.

Lawlessness Will Be Revealed
Evil will rise before judgment.

Perseverance Commended
God strengthens believers facing suffering.

Day of the Lord Clarified
The final day has not arrived yet.

Work Faithfully While Waiting
Believers must live responsibly each day.

1 TIMOTHY

KEY THEMES & HIGHLIGHTS

- ORDER IN THE CHURCH
- SOUND DOCTRINE PROTECTED
- GODLY LEADERSHIP STANDARDS
- FAITH EXPRESSED THROUGH CONDUCT

LIFE INSIDE GOD'S HOUSEHOLD

Healthy Teaching Matters
Truth protects the Church from error.

Care for Widows
The Church protects vulnerable members.

Qualified Church Leaders
Leaders must live above reproach.

Guidance for Worship
Public worship reflects reverence and order.

Guard the Gospel
Timothy must protect entrusted truth.

2 TIMOTHY

KEY THEMES & HIGHLIGHTS

- ⇨ **ENDURANCE IN MINISTRY**
- ⇨ **FAITHFULNESS TO SCRIPTURE**
- ⇨ **PASSING TRUTH FORWARD**
- ⇨ **FINISHING THE RACE**

A LIFE POURED OUT

Remain Loyal to Truth

Truth protects the Church from error.

Entrust Truth to Others

Faith must be passed faithfully.

Endure Courageously

Suffering is part of faithful service.

Scripture Equips Believers Fully

God's Word trains and corrects lives.

Await the Crown

Eternal reward awaits perseverance.

TITUS

KEY THEMES & HIGHLIGHTS

- ⇨ HEALTHY CHURCH LEADERSHIP
- ⇨ GRACE-DRIVEN TRANSFORMATION
- ⇨ GOOD WORKS FOLLOW FAITH
- ⇨ TRUTH LIVED OUT PUBLICLY

GRACE THAT SHAPES BEHAVIOR

Confront False Teaching
Error threatens healthy faith.

Grace Trains Believers
Godliness grows through discipline.

Appoint Faithful Elders
Leadership reflects sound teaching.

Grace Brings Salvation
Salvation comes from God's mercy.

Good Works Confirm Faith
Faith becomes visible through action.

PHILEMON

KEY THEMES & HIGHLIGHTS

- FORGIVENESS THROUGH CHRIST
- RECONCILIATION AND GRACE
- NEW IDENTITY IN CHRIST
- LOVE OVER SOCIAL STATUS

GRACE RESTORES RELATIONSHIPS

Onesimus Runs Away
A slave flees his Christian master.

Onesimus Meets Paul
He encounters the gospel message.

Paul Appeals for Mercy
Salvation comes from God's mercy.

Brotherhood in Christ
Status is transformed by faith.

Love Over Obligation
Grace reshapes relationships.

AT A GLANCE

Epistle	Main Theme	Date	Location
1 Thessalonians	Hope in Christ's return and encouragement	50–51	Corinth
2 Thessalonians	The Second Coming and steadfast faith	AD 51–52	Corinth
Galatians	Salvation by faith, not the Law	AD 53–55	Ephesus or Antioch
1 Corinthians	Unity, holiness, and order in the Church	AD 54–55	Ephesus
2 Corinthians	Apostolic authority, suffering, and reconciliation	AD 55–56	Macedonia
Romans	Salvation, grace, faith, and God's plan for all	AD 56–58	Corinth
Philippians	Joy, humility in Christ	AD 60–62	Rome
Colossians	Christ's supremacy	AD 60–62	Rome
Ephesians	Church as Christ's Body	AD 60–62	Rome
Philemon	Forgiveness and Christian brotherhood	AD 60–62	Rome
1 Timothy	Church leadership and sound teaching	AD 62–64	Macedonia
Titus	Order and discipline within the Church	AD 62–64	Macedonia or Nicopolis
2 Timothy	Perseverance and faithfulness until the end	AD 64–67	Rome (imprisoned

HEBREWS

KEY THEMES & HIGHLIGHTS

- CHRIST'S COMPLETE SUPERIORITY
- FAITHFUL PERSEVERANCE
- NEW COVENANT PROMISES
- ENDURING HOPE IN CHRIST

CHRIST OUR PERFECT HIGH PRIEST

Greater Than Angels
Christ surpasses all heavenly beings.

Perfect High Priest
Jesus intercedes forever.

Once-for-All Sacrifice
Sin is fully dealt with.

Call to Endurance
Faith must persevere through trials.

Witnesses Remembered
Past believers testify to faithfulness.

JAMES

KEY THEMES & HIGHLIGHTS

- FAITH PROVEN BY ACTION
- PRACTICAL GODLY WISDOM
- ENDURANCE THROUGH TRIALS
- CONTROLLED SPEECH

FAITH THAT ACTS

Ask God for Wisdom
God gives wisdom generously without criticism.

Control the Tongue
Words possess power to build or destroy.

Trials Refine Faith
Testing develops endurance and spiritual maturity.

Faith Requires Action
True faith reveals itself through obedience.

Care for the Vulnerable
True religion expresses compassion and integrity.

1 PETER

KEY THEMES & HIGHLIGHTS

- HOPE IN SUFFERING
- HOLY LIVING
- CHRIST'S EXAMPLE
- FUTURE GLORY

FAITH THAT ACTS

Called to Holiness
Believers reflect God's character in daily conduct.

Trust in God's Care
God remains sovereign amid trials.

Living Hope in Christ
Hope flows from Christ's resurrection and victory.

Suffering as Witness
Suffering follows Christ's example and purpose.

Glory to Come
Eternal reward awaits faithful believers.

2 PETER

KEY THEMES & HIGHLIGHTS

- SPIRITUAL GROWTH
- WARNING AGAINST FALSE TEACHERS
- GOD'S PROMISES
- CHRIST'S RETURN

GROWING TOWARD ETERNITY

False Teachers Exposed
False teaching leads people away from truth.

Trust in God's Care
God remains sovereign amid trials.

Grow in Godly Character
Faith matures through disciplined spiritual growth.

God's Promises Are Certain
God's timing never fails His word.

Glory to Come
Eternal reward awaits faithful believers.

1 JOHN

KEY THEMES & HIGHLIGHTS

- ⇨ RELATIONAL FELLOWSHIP WITH GOD
- ⇨ MORAL CLARITY
- ⇨ SPIRITUAL ASSURANCE
- ⇨ CHRIST-CENTERED BELIEF

LIFE SHAPED BY TRUE FELLOWSHIP

Restoration Through Confession

Admitting sin restores spiritual relationship with God.

Actions Reveal Inner Allegiance

Behavior confirms alignment with Christ's teaching.

God Reveals What Is True

Divine truth exposes deception and directs righteous living.

Love Reflects God's Nature

Authentic love demonstrates God's character within believers.

Confidence Rooted in Christ

Trust grows from remaining connected to Jesus.

2 JOHN

KEY THEMES & HIGHLIGHTS

- ⇨ FAITHFULNESS TO SOUND TEACHING
- ⇨ DISCERNMENT IN RELATIONSHIPS
- ⇨ OBEDIENT LOVE
- ⇨ DOCTRINAL PROTECTION

GUARDRAILS FOR THE CHURCH

Love Shown Through Obedience
Commitment to God shapes loving behavior.

Discernment Protects the Community
Careful boundaries preserve shared belief.

Truth Provides Direction
Sound teaching guides Christian relationships and decisions.

Deception Requires Vigilance
False teaching threatens spiritual stability.

Faithfulness Preserves Reward
Consistency safeguards spiritual fruit.

3 JOHN

KEY THEMES & HIGHLIGHTS

- FAITHFUL SUPPORT OF MINISTRY
- SPIRITUAL INTEGRITY
- HEALTHY CHURCH LEADERSHIP
- TRUTH-SHAPED REPUTATION

GUARDRAILS FOR THE CHURCH

Truth Shapes Reputation
Faithfulness becomes visible through consistent conduct.

Faithful Examples Inspire Others
Godly lives encourage imitation.

Strengthening Ministry
Supporting traveling teachers advances gospel work.

Authority Misused Causes Harm
Self-promotion disrupts church unity.

Discernment Guides Allegiance
Wisdom determines whom to follow.

JUDE

KEY THEMES & HIGHLIGHTS

- SPIRITUAL VIGILANCE
- DOCTRINAL FAITHFULNESS
- MORAL ACCOUNTABILITY
- DIVINE PRESERVATION

STANDING FIRM AGAINST CORRUPTION

Past Judgment as Warning

History reveals the consequences of rebellion.

Mercy Requires Discernment

Compassion must be guided by wisdom.

Corruption Enters Quietly

Ungodly influences distort truth from within.

Intentional Effort

Spiritual growth is strengthened through prayer and discipline.

God Secures His People

Believers remain upheld by divine power.

REVELATION

KEY THEMES & HIGHLIGHTS

- DIVINE SOVEREIGNTY
- ULTIMATE JUSTICE
- ENDURING HOPE
- ETERNAL RESTORATION

GOD'S PLAN FULFILLED

Christ Evaluates the Churches

Spiritual health is measured by faithfulness and perseverance.

Heaven Reveals Ultimate Authority

God governs history from His heavenly seat.

Evil Faces Decisive Judgment

God confronts rebellion through righteous acts.

Victory Brings Final Renewal

Evil is permanently removed from creation.

God Dwells with Humanity

Creation is restored to perfect communion.

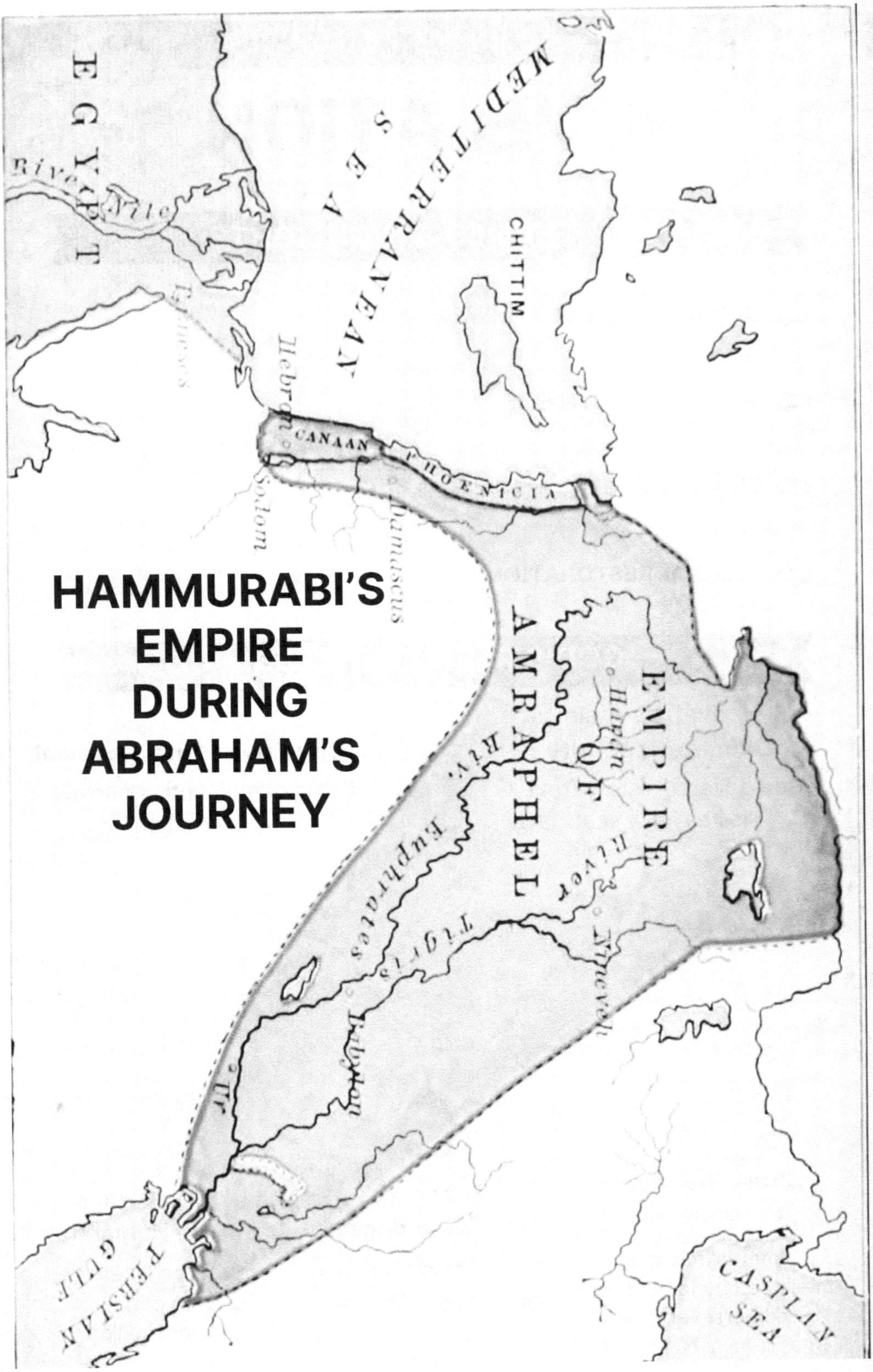

HAMMURABI'S EMPIRE DURING ABRAHAM'S JOURNEY

COMPARATIVE SIZE OF BIBLICAL MOUNTAINS

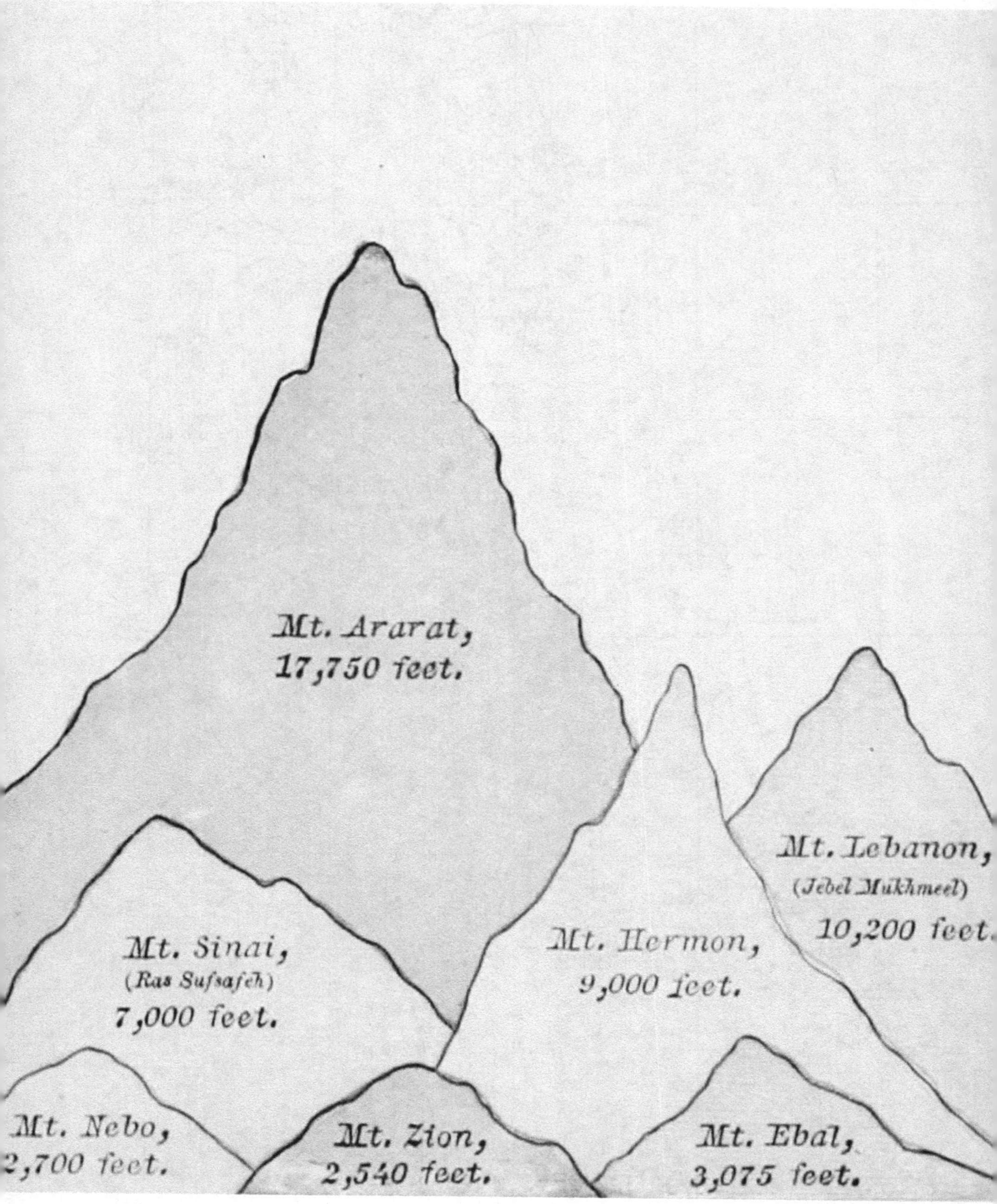

PALESTINE BEFORE ISRAEL

ISRAEL UNDER SAUL

ISRAEL UNDER DAVID

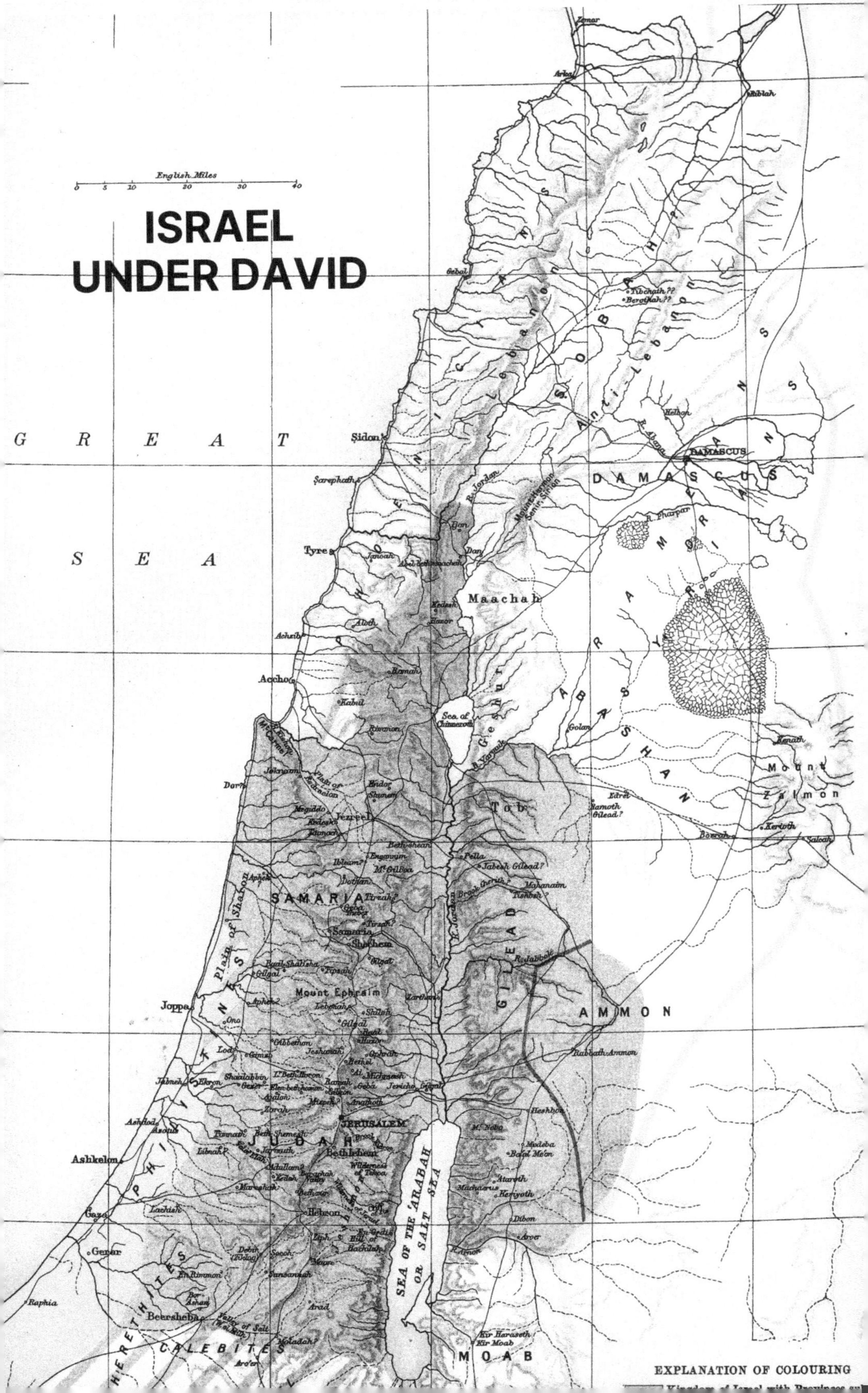

PLAN OF ANCIENT JERUSALEM

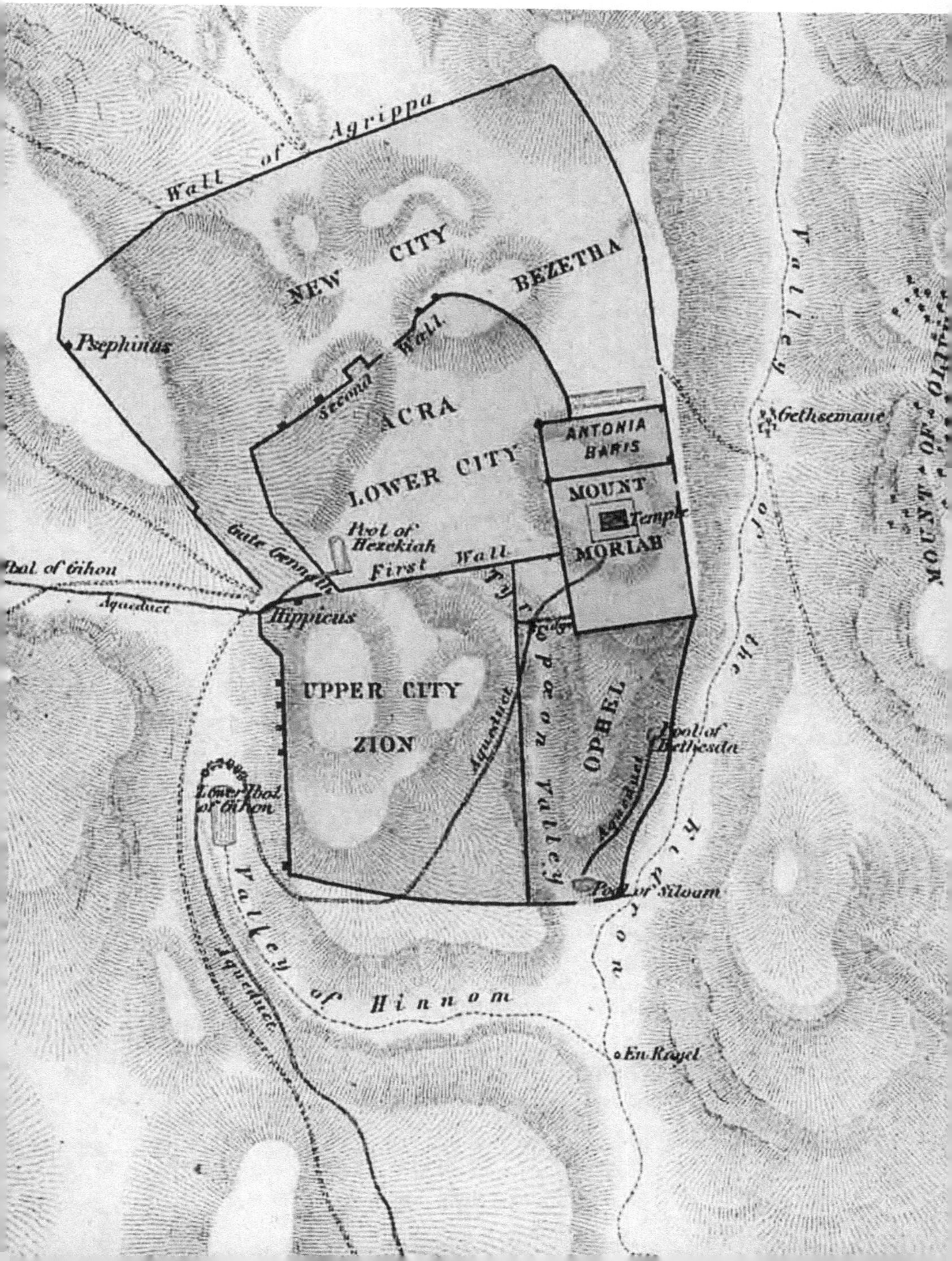

ISRAEL AND JUDAH DIVIDED

NATURAL FEATURES OF JERUSALEM

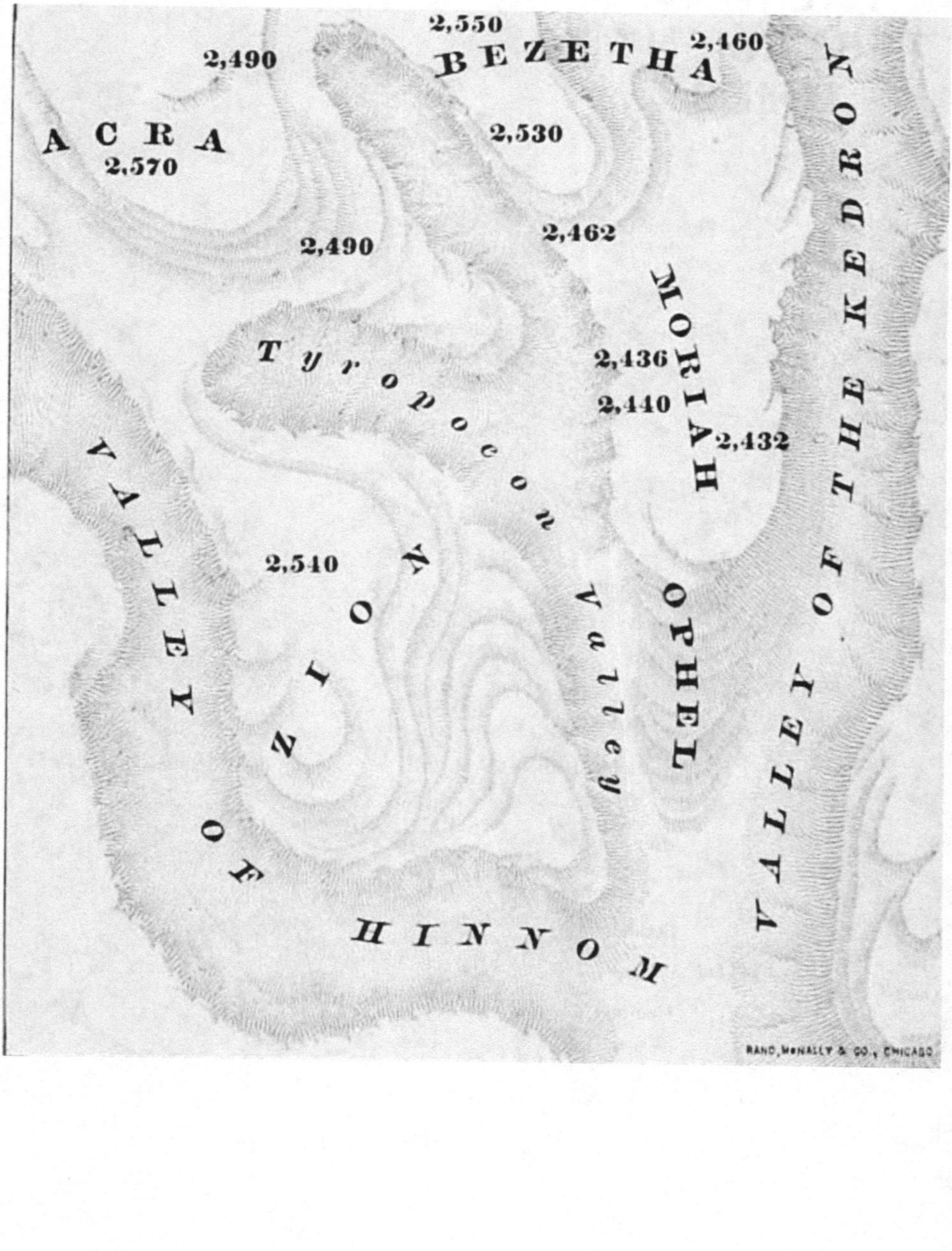

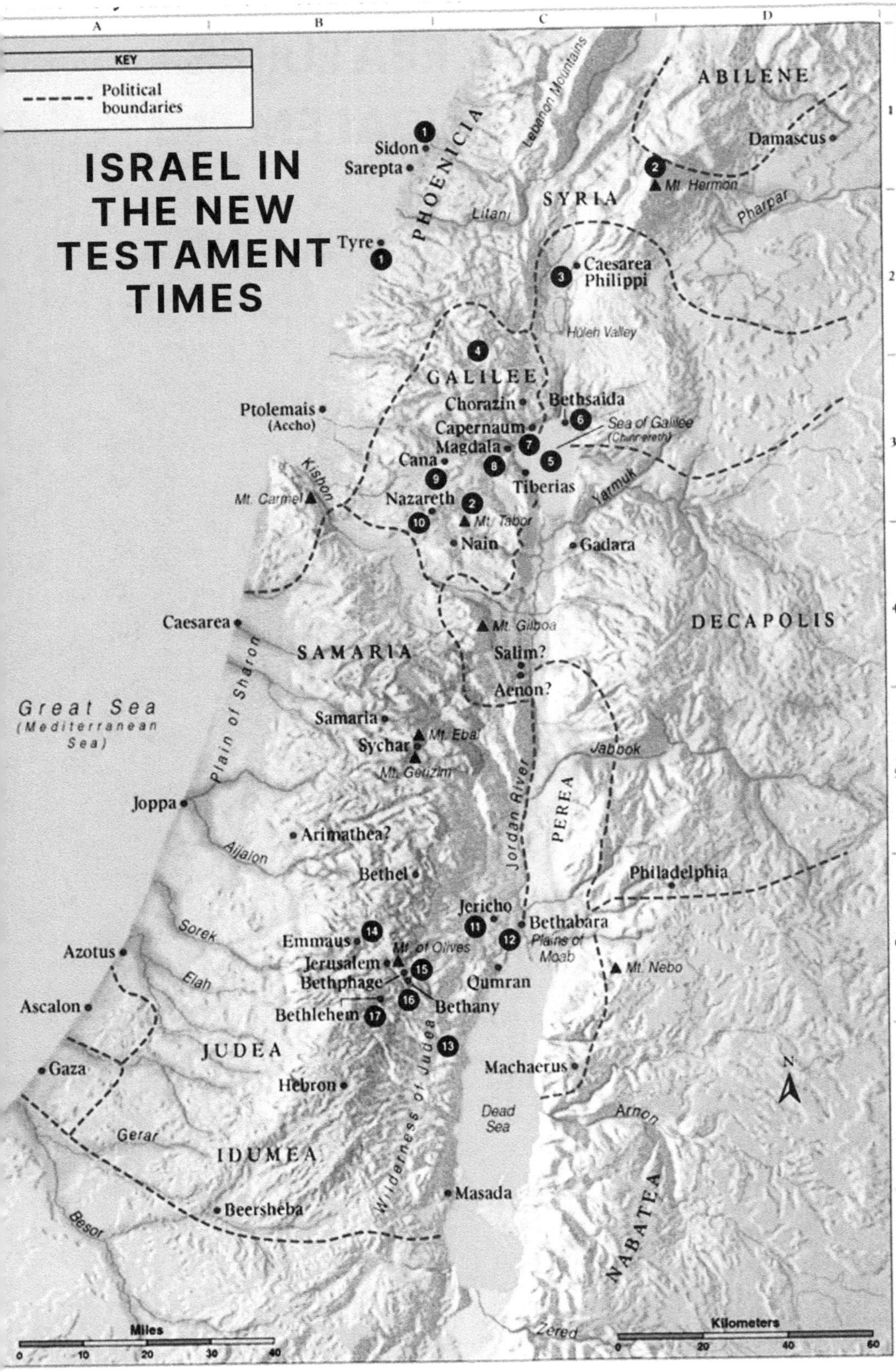
ISRAEL IN THE NEW TESTAMENT TIMES
KEY
Political boundaries
A
B
C
D
1
2
3
4
5
6
7
8
ABILENE
PHOENICIA
SYRIA
GALILEE
SAMARIA
DECAPOLIS
PEREA
JUDEA
IDUMEA
NABATEA
Great Sea (Mediterranean Sea)
Lebanon Mountains
Sidon
Sarepta
Tyre
Litani
Damascus
Mt. Hermon
Pharpar
Caesarea Philippi
Hulen Valley
Chorazin
Bethsaida
Capernaum
Sea of Galilee (Chinnereth)
Magdala
Cana
Tiberias
Yarmuk
Ptolemais (Accho)
Kishon
Mt. Carmel
Nazareth
Mt. Tabor
Nain
Gadara
Caesarea
Mt. Gilboa
Salim?
Aenon?
Plain of Sharon
Samaria
Mt. Ebal
Sychar
Mt. Gerizim
Jabbok
Jordan River
Joppa
Arimathea?
Aijalon
Bethel
Philadelphia
Jericho
Bethabara
Plains of Moab
Sorek
Emmaus
Mt. of Olives
Azotus
Jerusalem
Bethphage
Qumran
Mt. Nebo
Elah
Ascalon
Bethlehem
Bethany
Gaza
Machaerus
Hebron
Wilderness of Judea
Dead Sea
Arnon
Gerar
Masada
Beersheba
Besor
Zered
Miles
0 10 20 30 40
Kilometers
0 20 40 60
N

NATURAL FEATURES OF JERUSALEM

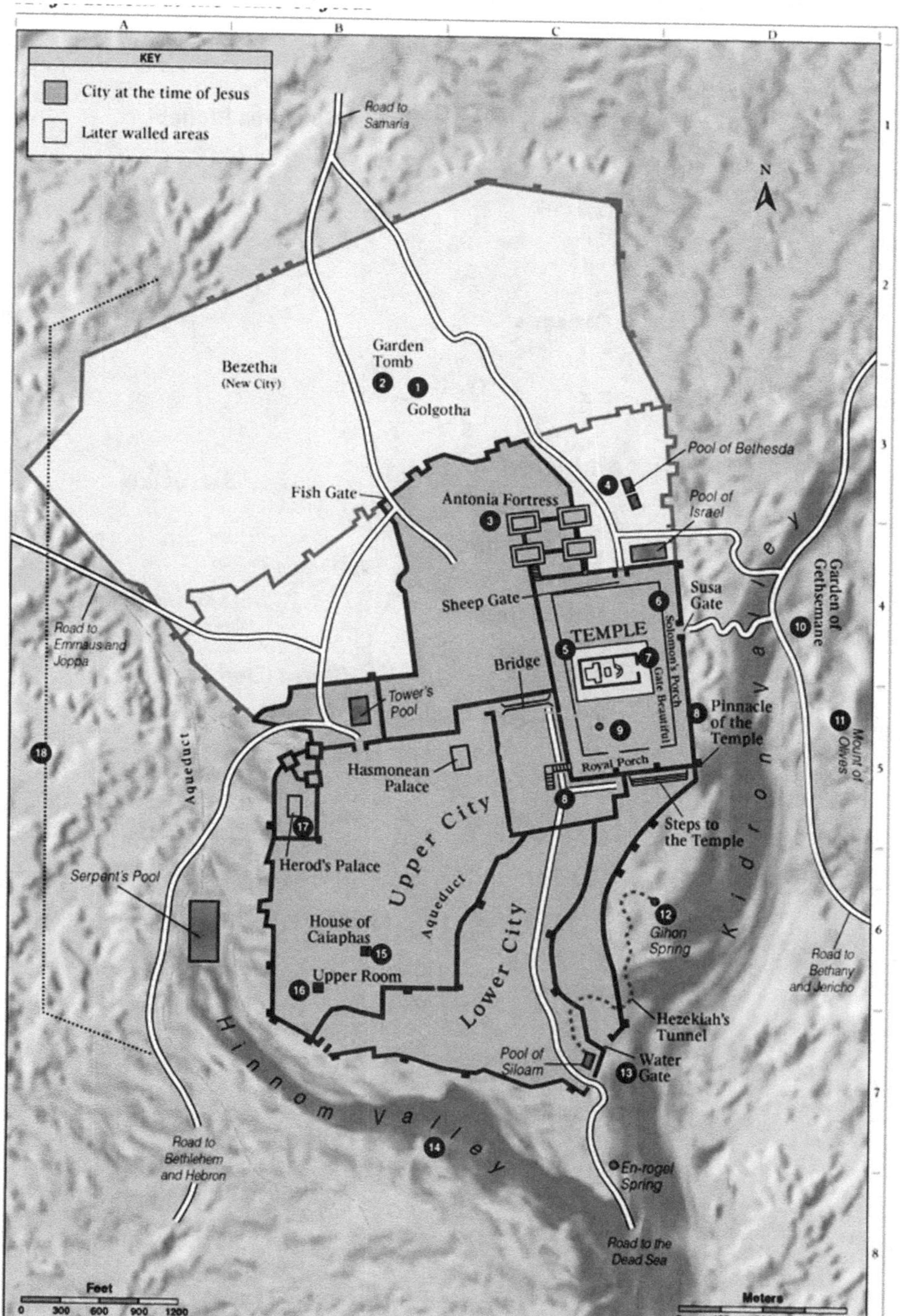

JESUS' GALILEAN MINISTRY

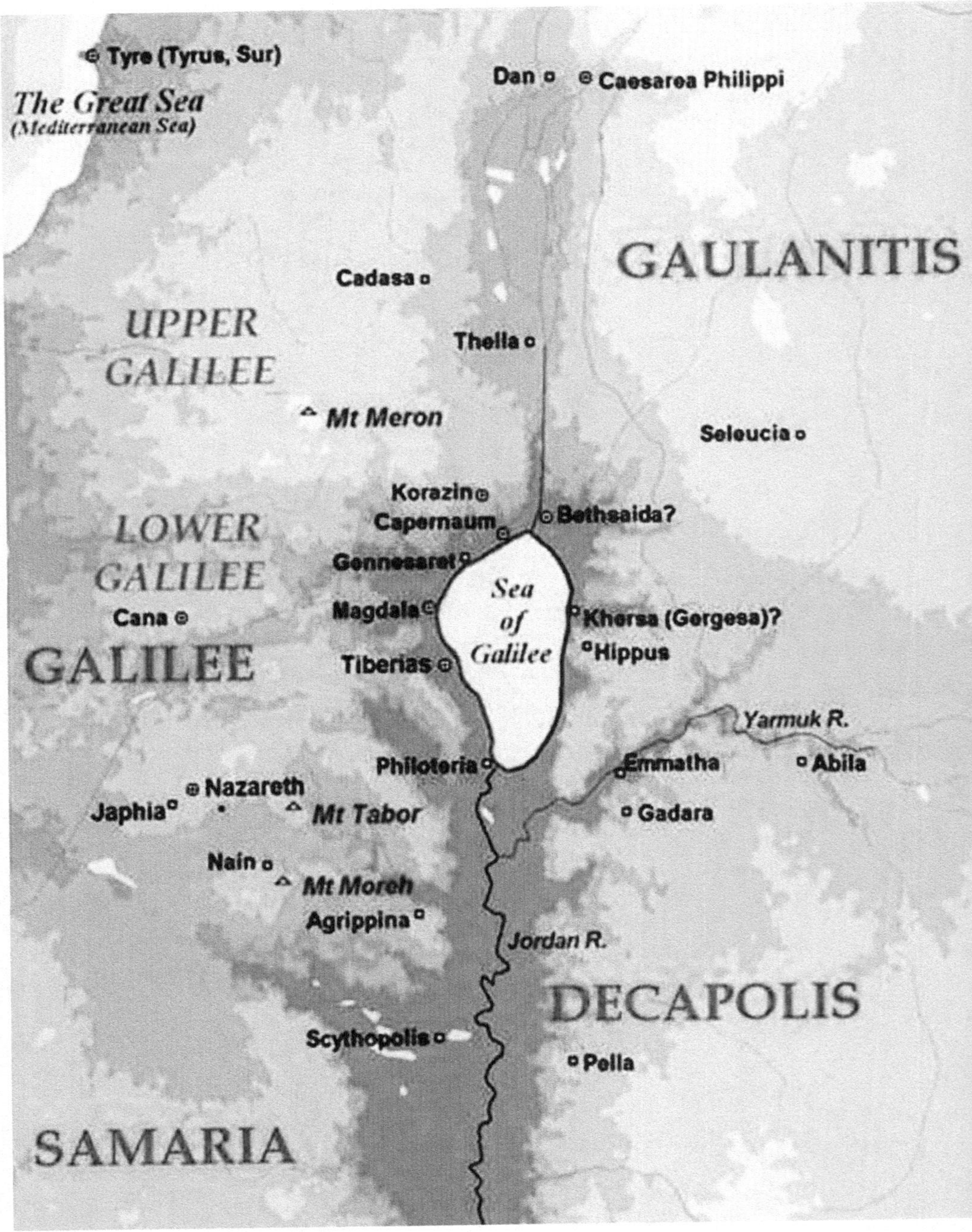

THE ISLAND OF CYPRUS

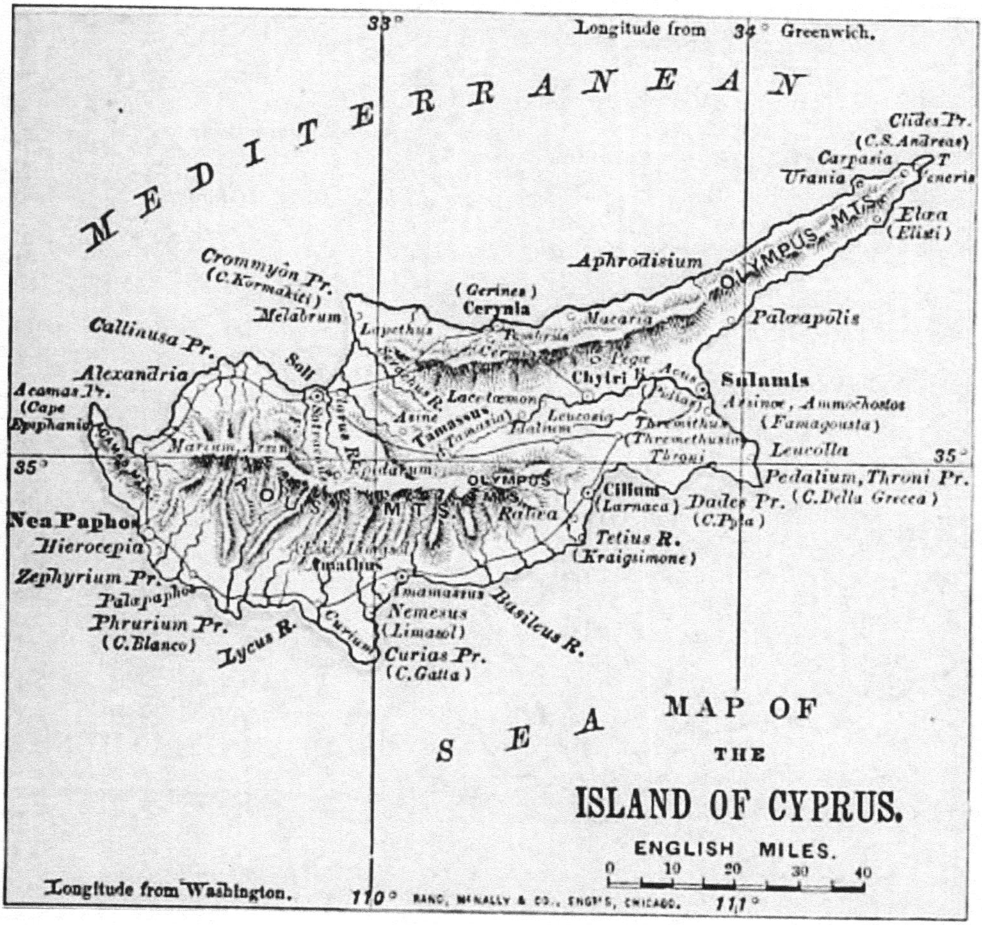

THE CITY OF ATHENS

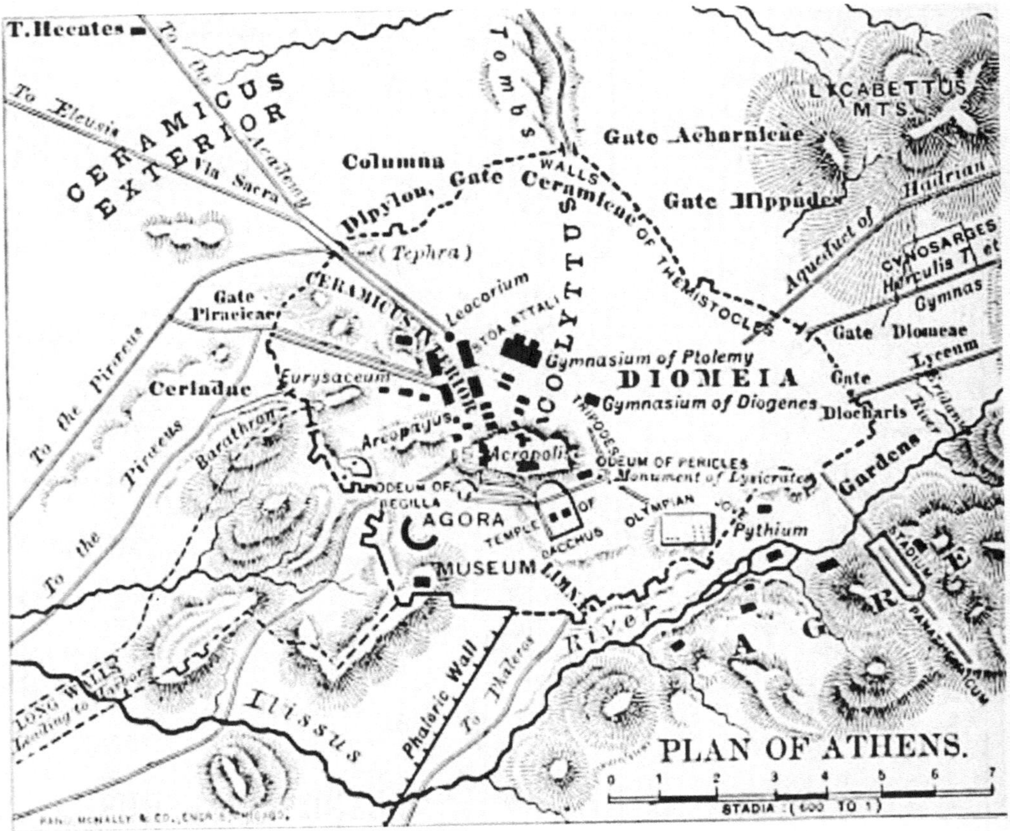

ST. PAUL'S BAY, MALTA

PAUL'S MISSIONARY JOURNEYS

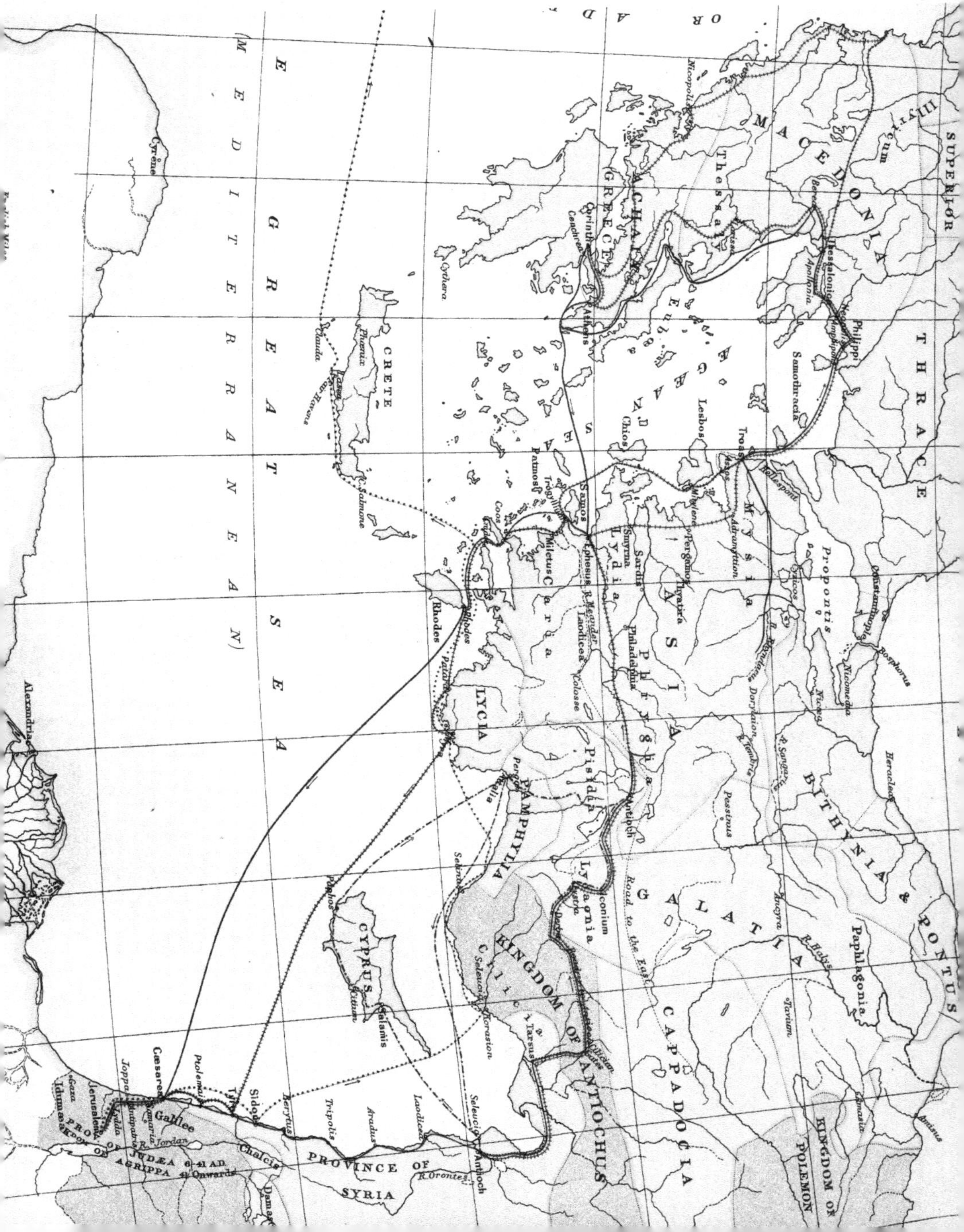

THE MODERN MIDDLE EAST

ILLUSTRATIONS

BIRS NIMROUD
(SUPPOSED TOWER OF BABEL)

MT ARARAT

MT TABOR

THE JEWS' WAILING PLACE,
AT JERUSALEM.

JERICHO AND THE JORDAN

MT SINAI

TOWER OF DAVID

DAVID'S TOMB

SOLOMON'S POOLS

GARDEN OF GETHSEMANE

SHECHEM

HEBRON

TIBERIAS

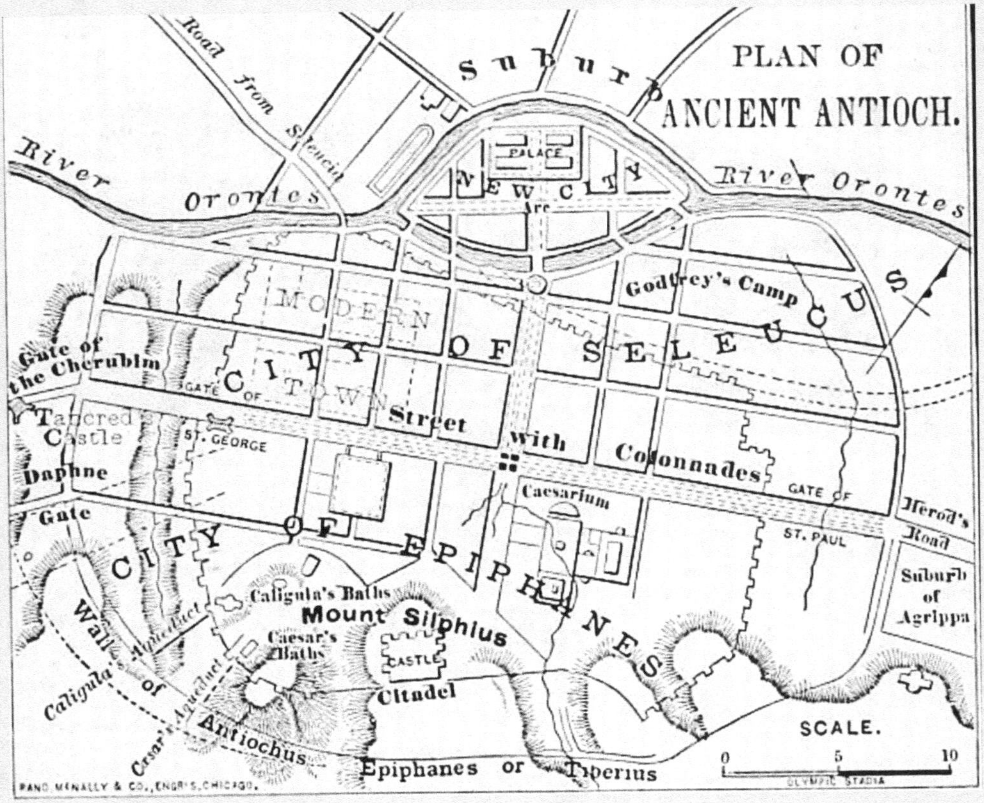

ANCIENT ANTIOCH

SYRIAN ANTIOCH

THE ACROPOLIS AT ATHENS
(AREOPAGUS ON THE LEFT)

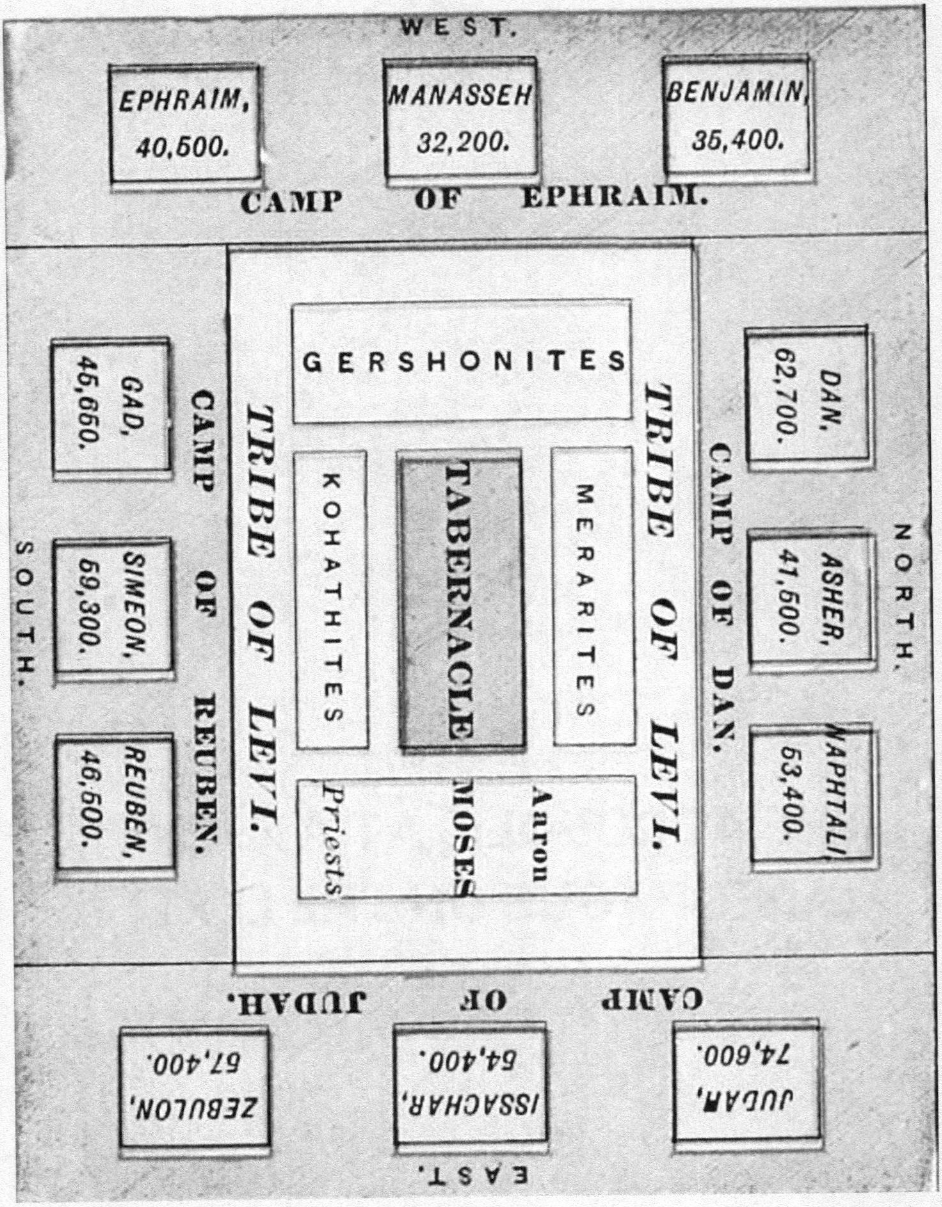

THE CAMP OF ISRAEL

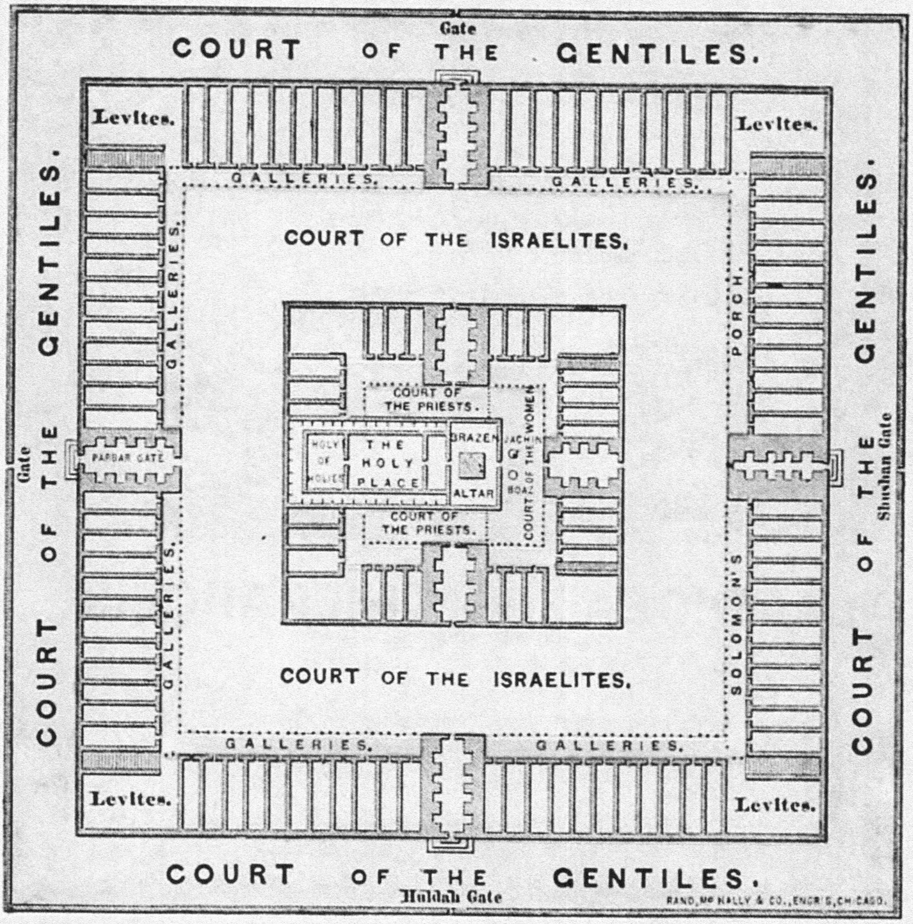

LAYOUT OF SOLOMON'S TEMPLE

LAODICEA FROM HIERAPOLIS

BETHANY

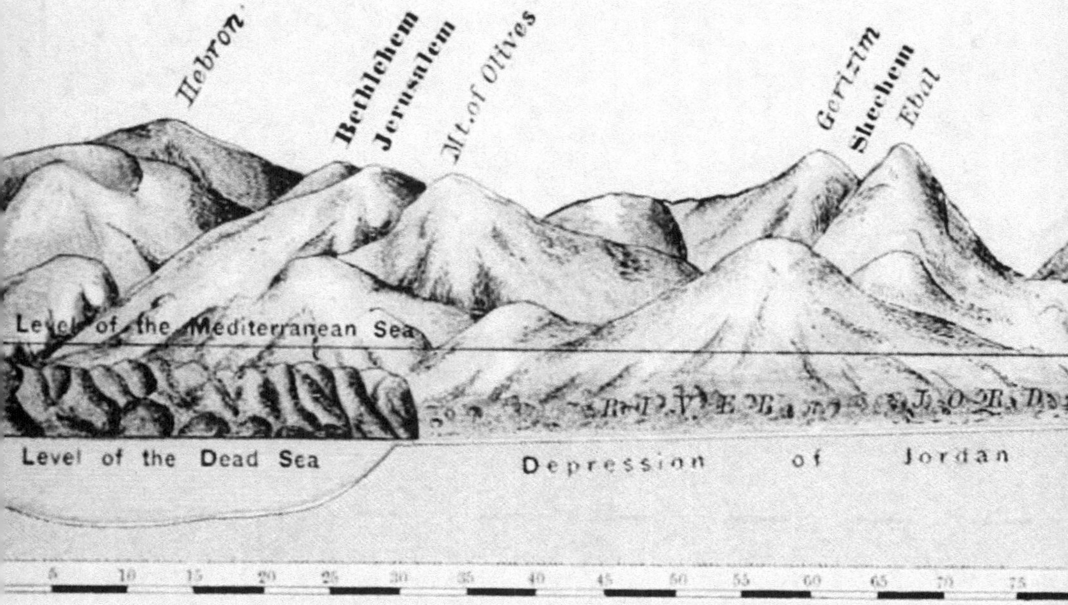

PALESTINE FROM

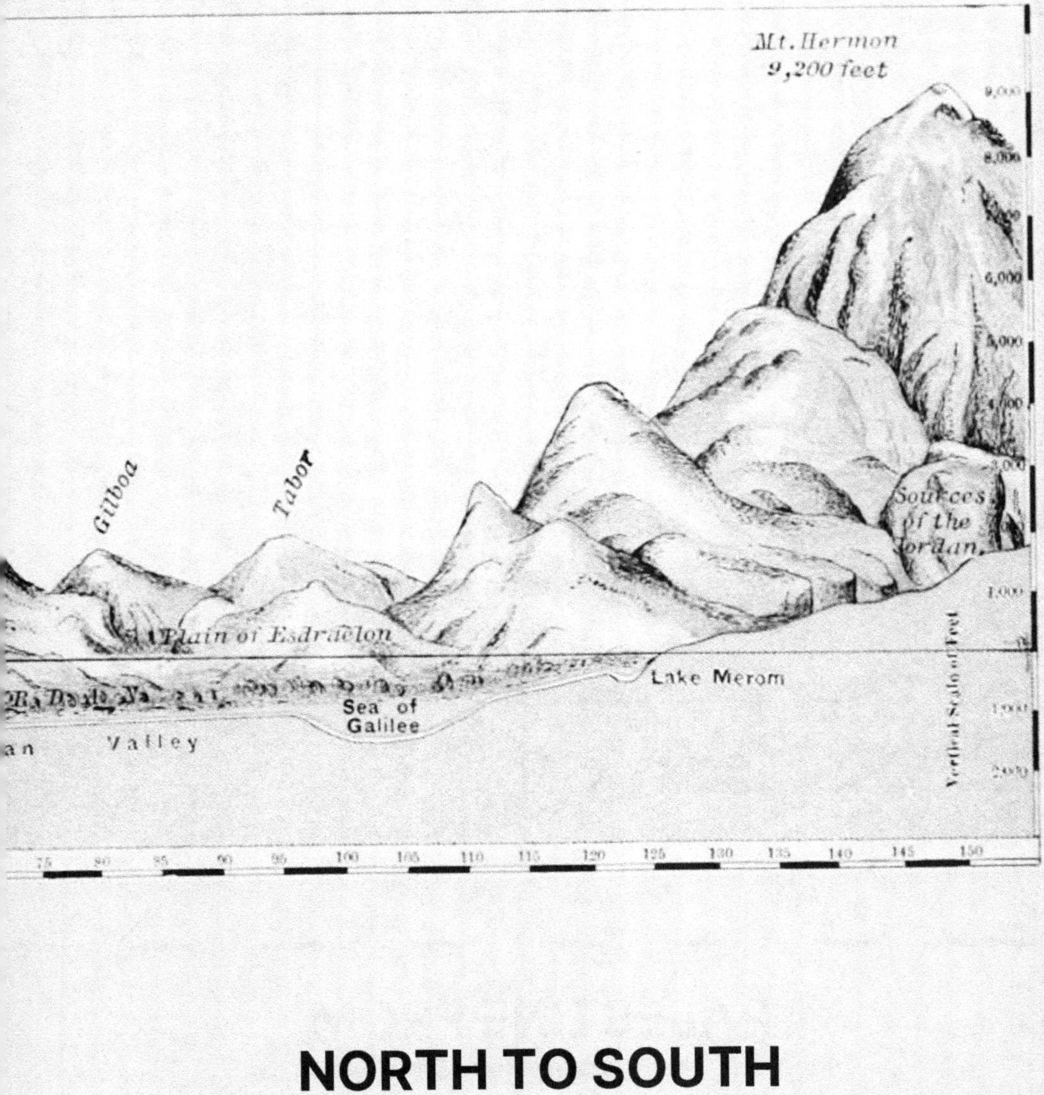

NORTH TO SOUTH

WEEKLY BIBLE
READING TRACKER

Track your spiritual journey and grow in faith day by day.

PERSONAL INFO

Name: ______________________________

Start Date: ______________________________

Goal (e.g., read entire Bible in a year): ______________________________

WEEKLY SCHEDULE

Monday: ______________________________

Tuesday: ______________________________

Wednesday: ______________________________

Thursday: ______________________________

Friday: ______________________________

Saturday: ______________________________

Sunday: ______________________________

BOOKS READ

- Genesis
- Exodus
- Leviticus
- Numbers
- Deuteronomy
- Joshua
- Judges
- Ruth
- 1 Samuel
- 2 Samuel
- 1 Kings
- 2 Kings
- 1 Chronicles
- 2 Chronicles
- Ezra
- Nehemiah
- Tobit
- Judith
- Esther
- Job
- Psalms
- Proverbs
- Ecclesiastes
- Song of Songs
- Wisdom
- Sirach
- Isaiah
- Jeremiah
- Lamentations
- Baruch
- Ezekiel
- Daniel
- Hosea
- Joel
- Amos
- Obadiah
- Jonah
- Micah
- Nahum
- Habakkuk
- Zephaniah
- Haggai
- Zechariah
- Malachi
- 1 Maccabees
- 2 Maccabees
- Matthew
- Mark
- Luke
- John
- Acts
- Romans
- 1 Corinthians
- 1 Timothy
- 2 Timothy
- Titus
- Philemon
- Hebrews
- James
- 1 Peter
- 2 Peter
- 1 John
- 2 John
- 3 John
- Jude
- Revelation

MONTHLY PROGRESS REVIEW

Month: ______________________________

Books Completed: ______________________________

Chapters Read: ______________________________

Spiritual Growth Notes: ______________________________

____

DAILY DEVOTIONAL

Date: ____________________

Bible Verse

____

My observation: ____________________

____

____

____

____

____

My reflection: ____________________

____

____

Personal prayer: ____________________

____

____

I will apply this for: __________

____

____

____

I am thankful for: __________

____

____

____